Counselling and Psychotherapy

(Strictly on the basis of prescribed syllabus with modern trends)

Counselling and Psychotherapy

(Strictly on the basis of prescribed syllabus with modern trends)

Medha Vasishit

AUTHORSPRESS

Worldwide Circulation through Authorspress Global Network
First Published 2008
by
Authorspress
E-35/103, Jawahar Park
Laxmi Nagar, Delhi-110 092
e-mail: authorspress@yahoo.com

Counselling and Psychotherapy
ISBN 978-81-7273-466-4

Printed in India at Virgo Press, Delhi.

Preface

In a world increasingly defined by ever-growing emotional disorders and problems in living, psychotherapy has emerged as an effective solution to cope with these challenges. Psychotherapy is a form of treatment in which the therapist, through talking with the patient, attempts to help him or her confront issues, primarily emotional in nature, and overcome the difficulties associated with them. These 'issues' include several psychoses and neuroses, such as phobias, anxiety reactions, depression, obsessions, compulsive behaviour, as well as interpersonal difficulties as unassertiveness, lack of interpersonal skill, violent behaviour, deviant sexual behaviour, marital and family difficulties, and even habit problems like drug abuse, excessive and obesity. As such, the benefits of psychotherapy cannot be overemphasised, and there is great need for active encouragement of this process.

This text, written for those pursuing their Masters in Education, attempts to acquaint readers with the processes and practices which define counselling and psychotherapy in the modern age. Guiding the readers upon the objectives and features of psychotherapy, the book explores the formats of psychotherapy, based upon a broad discussion of the different schools and theories of the subject. The role of the therapist in the process of the patient's treatment has been effectively emphasised upon, with a detailed analysis of current therapies which give shape to this role. The approach of the book is highly incisive, with the content moulded in such a manner that it fosters a thorough comprehension of the ways in which psychotherapy impacts people's lives. The challenges and issues regarding counselling have also been addressed, along with critical perspectives which allow readers to understand the importance of psychotherapy even better.

It is hoped that the book proves to be an incisive and erudite text for all.

Medha Vasishit

Contents

1

Introduction to Counselling and Psychotherapy

1.1. Introduction

Counselling can be defined as a relatively short-term, interpersonal, theory-based process of helping persons who are fundamentally psychologically healthy resolve developmental and situational issues. It is an activity that takes place when someone who is troubled invites and allows another person to enter into a particular kind of relationship with them. A person seeks such a relationship when they encounter a 'problem in living' that they have not been able to resolve through their everyday resources, and that has resulted in their exclusion from some aspect of full participation in social life.

Counselling has a vast meaning in this era. In this complex, busy and changing world, it is hard to lead a calm and quiet life. Now, there are many different types of experience that are difficult for people to cope with. Most of the time, we get on with life, but sometimes we are stopped in our tracks by an event or situation that we do not, at that moment, have the resources to sort out. Most of the time, we find ways of dealing with such problems in living by talking to family, friends, neighbours, priests or our family doctor. But occasionally their advice is not sufficient, or we are too embarrassed or ashamed to tell them what is bothering us, or we just don't have an appropriate person to turn to.

Counselling is a really useful option at these moments. In most places, counselling is available fairly quickly, and costs little or nothing. The counsellor does not diagnose or label you, but does his or her best to listen to you and work with you to find the best ways to understand and resolve your problem.

Counselling profession is also very dignified and rewarding job. Counsellors are those who make a profound difference to the life of another human being. It is always a great privilege to be allowed to be a witness and companion to someone who is facing their own worst fears and dilemmas. It is also challenging and is always more to learn. The role of counsellor lends itself to flexible work arrangements. There are excellent counsellors who are full-time paid staff; others who work for free in the evenings for voluntary agencies; and some who are able sensitively to offer a counselling relationship within other work roles, such as nurse, doctor, clergy, social worker or teacher.

1.1.1. A Panacea for Mental Illness

Counselling is not just for "the mentally ill." Today, many individuals and families are seeking professional help to deal with the trauma of life in a fallen world. People typically enter counselling and psychotherapy because they are hurting, frustrated, or feeling overwhelmed by a problem. In most cases, difficult circumstances drive the felt need for counselling. Most of these circumstances are based in wounded relationships between husbands and wives and parents and children. And, of course, one or more persons in these relationships may be experiencing intrapersonal difficulties, including mood disorders like depression and anxiety, addictions, or situational stressors like work or school.

Counselling and therapy can be helpful for most situations involving psychological, emotional, relationship, parenting, family and employment problems. There is significant risk of harm to your health, well being, reputation, personal freedom and future if you participate in psychotherapy or counselling with an unlicensed unsupervised person. You will get more out of therapy if you are informed, educate yourself and take an active (rather than passive) role in finding and selecting your counsellor or psychotherapist.

Mental illness is a sickness which needs a long period to cure. Mostly, it requires a minimum of 3 to 6 months of counselling or psychotherapy to produce a lasting benefit. Very few problems or conditions require more than 1 year. In most cases, psychotherapy is self-limiting for most major disorders and problems. However, many people will continue therapy or counselling for personal growth, relapse prevention and for support for more than a year. Medications for emotional and psychological problems should be avoided unless (a) they are medically necessary, (b) there is no other acceptable alternative, and (c) the risk of taking (or not taking) medications is fully understood.

1.2. Origin of Counselling and Psychotherapy

Sigmund Freud is the biggest contributor to the psychological therapies. However, many modern approaches to counselling and psychotherapy are now much more firmly grounded in other bodies of thought.

Modern psychological therapies trace their history back to the work of Sigmund Freud in Vienna in the 1880s. Trained as a neurologist, Freud entered private practice in 1886 and by 1896 had developed a method of working with hysterical patients which he called 'psychoanalysis'. Others such as Alfred Adler, Snador Ferenczi, Karl Abraham and Otto Rank were also analysed by Freud and had brief apprentice-type training from him before becoming psychoanalysts in their own right.

In the early 1900s, Ernest Jones and A.A. Brill, from the UK and US respectively, visited Freud in Vienna and returned to their own countries to promote Freud's methods; Freud himself began a lecture tour of North America in 1909. Gradually many such as Ferenczi, Adler, Rank, Stekel and Reich began to develop their own theories and approaches, which sometimes differed markedly from Freud's. Jung in particular, a close collaborator of Freud's from 1907-1913 who was in some sense 'groomed' as Freud's intellectual successor, eventually split from Freud and pursued the development of his own school of analytical psychology, drawing heavily on both Freud's and Adler's ideas. All these immediate descendants of Freud's approach are characterised by a focus on the dynamics of the relationships between different parts of the psyche and the external world; thus the term 'psychodynamics'.

A separate strand of psychological therapies developed later under the influence of psychology and learning theory and leading thinkers such as B.F. Skinner. Rejecting the notion of 'hidden' aspects of the psyche which cannot be examined empirically, practitioners in the behavioural tradition began to focus on what could actually be observed in the outside world.

Finally, under the influence of Adler and Rank, a 'third way' was pioneered by the US psychologist Carl Rogers. Originally called 'client-centred' and later 'person-centred', Rogers's approach focuses on the experience of the person, neither adopting elaborate and empirically untestable theoretical constructs of the type common in psychodynamic traditions, nor neglecting the internal world of the client in the way of early behaviourists. Other approaches also developed under what came to be called the 'humanistic' branch of psychotherapy, including Gestalt therapy and the psychodrama of J.L. Moreno. The figure below illustrates some of the historical links between these three main strands which developed from Freud's original contributions.

Competent counselling and psychotherapy can offer viable alternatives to psychiatric medications. Any person's ability to benefit from counselling or psychotherapy will be less certain if you rely on managed health care to authorise and restrict the services you receive. Managed health care has a tremendous influence and impact on the practice patterns of professionals. Managed care will also attempt to influence and limit your treatment. Using managed health care has many indirect impacts.

1.2.1. Symptoms of Mental Illness

— Depression, mood swings, anxiety or loneliness

— Excessive anger, frustration or guilt

— Constant worries or obsessions

— Problems with food, alcohol or other drug use

— Changes or potential changes in your life

— Problems following an abusive or a traumatic event

— Communication problems

— Marital, parenting, employment or relationship problems

— Health problems, sleep problems, or medical symptoms worsened by a psychological problem

— A crisis that involves self-harming behaviour, a risk of violence or the risk of suicide

1.2.2. Healing Methods

Counselling is a way of addressing and resolving issues. It can involve identifying options and choosing between them, learning new skills to cope better with problems, gaining greater understanding of what is occurring, or being supported while recovering from some significant life event.

Counselling is a collaborative process that involves the development of a unique, confidential helping relationship. The counsellor acts as a facilitator in helping clients to understand feelings, behaviours, relationships with others, situations, choices and decisions. Further, the counsellor offers a safe, confidential and non-judgmental context in which clients can:

— Gain clarity and perspective on the issue;

— Receive the support they need to resolve issues and make decisions;

— Deal with negative feelings and emotions;

— Explore personal resources and develop new skills.

The overall aim of counselling is to enable people to work towards living their lives in a more positive and satisfying way. It is a form of helping based upon 'listening.'

Counselling provides people with an opportunity to explore their life issues in regular sessions within a confidential and safe setting. Furthermore, people may be emotionally troubled due to current life circumstances or life events and may often suffer from stress, anxiety or depression as a result.

1.3. Types of Counselling

1.3.1. 'One to One' Supportive Counselling

In this type, a depressed person gets a patient mind to hear your worries over with in privacy, knowing that what you say is confidential. You may have some practical issues that you want help in sorting out. The counsellor may not use a particular counselling method here. But they're a trained person who will listen to you, and help you work out some solutions. This can be very helpful.

1.3.2. Cognitive Behavioural Therapy (CBT)

It is a mental process that people use to remember, reason, understand, problem solve and judge things. Behaviour describes your actions or reactions to something. CBT aims to help you change how you respond to situations or emotions. It helps you understand how your thought patterns may be contributing to feeling depression or fear. This therapy also teaches you how to calm your body and mind. This helps you to control your feelings more, think more clearly and generally feel better about things.

1.3.3. Group Counselling

Group counselling, sometimes called 'group therapy,' means joining in a group where everyone discusses their problems together. Usually, everyone in the group is facing similar problems, but not always. The counsellor will facilitate the group and encourage people to express their feelings within it. Some people find it very helpful to learn that they are not alone with their worries. But this method doesn't suit everyone, especially if you have some very personal and painful issues you want to discuss.

1.3.4. Family Counselling

If you are affected by chronic illness, it also affects your family members also. So, the family members may be too scared to express to you how they really feel about your illness. You may not feel well enough or have the time to sit and talk honestly with your partner and children. Talking to children about cancer can be very difficult and upsetting. Having the support of a family counsellor may help make these things easier.

Children may be keeping a lot of their feelings to themselves for fear of upsetting you. They're likely to be trying to deal with your illness as well as keeping up with schoolwork, looking after younger siblings and wanting to feel supported and accepted by friends.

Teenage is the period of endless problems. Teenagers often feel confused and unsure about themselves anyway. This can make the way they deal with a parent's illness very different to that of a younger child. And their reactions are likely to be more intense than an adult's. It's very important that they have the time to grieve about the illness and be included in what's happening. They may become anxious, angry, moody, depressed or pretend that they're coping very well when actually inside they're feeling very scared and lonely. Equally many teenagers behave in a mature and supportive way, and remain or become very close to their parents.

1.4. Objectives of Counselling

The following are some of the objectives of counselling:

1.4.1. Insight

The acquisition of an understanding of the origins and development of emotional difficulties, leading to an increased capacity to take rational control over feelings and actions.

1.4.2. Relating with Others

Becoming better able to form and maintain meaningful and satisfying relationships with other people: for example, within the family or workplace.

1.4.3. Self-Awareness

Becoming more aware of thoughts and feelings that had been blocked off or denied, or developing a more accurate sense of how self is perceived by others.

1.4.4. Self-Acceptance

The development of a positive attitude towards self, marked by an ability to acknowledge areas of experience that had been the subject of self-criticism and rejection.

1.4.5. Self-Actualisation or Individuation

Moving in the direction of fulfilling potential or achieving an integration of previously conflicting parts of self.

1.4.6. Enlightenment

Assisting the client to arrive at a higher state of spiritual awakening.

1.4.7. Problem-Solving

Finding a solution to a specific problem that the client had not been able to resolve alone.

1.4.8. Psychological Education

Enabling the client to acquire ideas and techniques with which to understand and control behaviour.

1.4.9. Acquisition of Social Skills

Learning and mastering social and interpersonal skills such as maintenance of eye contact, turn-taking in conversations, assertiveness or anger control.

1.4.10. Cognitive Change

The modification or replacement of irrational beliefs or maladaptive thought patterns associated with self-destructive behaviour.

1.4.11. Behaviour Change

The modification or replacement of maladaptive or selfdestructive patterns of behaviour.

1.4.12. Empowerment

Working on skills, awareness and knowledge that will enable the client to take control of his or her own life.

1.4.13. Restitution

Helping the client to make amends for previous destructive behaviour.

1.4.14. Generativity and Social Action

Inspiring in the person a desire and capacity to care for others and pass on knowledge (generativity) and to contribute to the collective good through political engagement and community work.

Psychodynamic counsellors have focused primarily on insight, humanistic practitioners have aimed to promote self-acceptance and personal freedom, and cognitive-behavioural therapists have been mainly concerned with the management and control of behaviour. However, any valid counselling approach should be flexible enough to make it possible for the client to use the therapeutic relationship as an arena for exploring whatever dimension of life is most relevant to their well-being at that point in time.

1.5. Diversity in Counselling

Counselling is not merely a process of individual learning. It is also a social activity that has a social meaning, Often, people turn to counselling at a point of transition, such as the transition from child to adult, married to divorced, addict to straight. Counselling is also a culturally sanctioned means of enabling adaptation to social institutions. Counsellors are rarely managers or executives who hold power in colleges, businesses or communities. Counsellors, instead, have a more 'liminal' role, being employed at the edge of these institutions to deal with those in danger of falling off or falling out.

The three major emotional and behavioural problems of human beings are psychodynamic, cognitive-behavioural and humanistic. The mix of cultural, economic and social forces that contributed to the emergence of a multiplicity of counselling theories has also given rise to a wide diversity of settings where counselling is practised and client groups at whom it is targeted.

There are, for example, many counselling agencies that are funded by, or attached to, organisations that have a primary task of providing medical and health care. These range from mental health/psychiatric settings, which typically deal with highly disturbed or damaged clients, through to counselling available in primary care settings, such as GP surgeries, and from community nurses. There has been a growth in specialist counselling directed towards people with particular medical conditions such as AIDS, cancer and various genetic disorders.

1.5.1. Importance of Counselling in a Tensed World

Counselling has also played an important role in many centres and clinics offering alternative or complementary health approaches. One of the primary cultural locations for counselling and psychotherapy can therefore be seen to be alongside medicine. Even when counsellors and counselling agencies work independently of medical organisations, they will frequently establish some form of liaison with medical and psychiatric services, to enable referral of clients who may require medical or nursing care.

Today, the counsellors has high demand for helping people through difficulties, dilemmas or anxieties concerning their work role. These agencies include vocational guidance, student counselling services and employee assistance programmes or workplace counselling provided by large organisations in industry and the public sector. Whether the work role is that of executive, postal worker or college student, counsellors are able to offer help with stress and anxiety arising from the work, coping with change and making career decisions. There is yet another whole section of counselling practice that is not primarily focused on arriving at solutions to problems, but is instead directed towards the exploration of meaning and the expansion of awareness. This kind of counselling is strongly represented in private practice and 'growth centres.'

Counsellors and organisations are very active in the areas of marital breakdown, rape and bereavement. The work of the counsellor in these agencies can very clearly be seen as arising from social problems. For example, changing social perceptions of marriage, redefinitions of male and female roles, new patterns of marriage and family life, and legislation making divorce more available represent major social and cultural changes of the past century.

Counselling provides a way of helping individuals to negotiate this changing social landscape. A further field of counselling activity lies in the area of addictions. There exists a range of counselling approaches developed to help people with problems related to drug and alcohol abuse, food addiction and smoking cessation. The social role of the counsellor can be seen particularly clearly in this type of work. In some areas of addiction counselling, such as with hard drug users, counsellors operate alongside a set of powerful legal constraints and moral judgements.

The incidence of alcohol- and smoking-related diseases would be more effectively reduced by tax increases than by increases in the number of counsellors, an insight that raises questions about the role of counselling in relation to other means of control of behaviour.

1.5.2. Scope of Counselling as an Area of Study

Counselling and psychotherapy was initially emerged from within the discipline of psychiatry. But today, they are considering as applied sub-branches of the academic discipline of psychology. In some European countries, holding a psychology degree is necessary to enter training in psychotherapy.

The concept of the 'unconscious' had been used in nineteenth-century philosophy some time before Freud began to use it in his theory. The concepts of phenomenology and authenticity had been developed by existential philosophers such as Heidegger and Husserl long before they influenced Rogers, Perls and other humanistic therapists. The field of moral philosophy also makes an input into counselling, by offering a framework for making sense of ethical issues.

Religion also has a strong influence on counselling theory and practice. Several counselling agencies have either begun their life as branches of the church or been helped into existence by founders with a religious calling. Many of the key figures in the history of counselling and psychotherapy have had strong religious backgrounds, and have attempted to integrate the work of the counsellor with the search for spiritual meaning. Jung has made the most significant contribution in this area. Although the field of counselling is permeated with Judaeo-Christian thought and belief, there is increasing interest among some counsellors in the relevance of ideas and practices from other religions, such as Zen Buddhism.

There is a strong tradition in counselling and psychotherapy of using methods and techniques from drama, sculpture, dance and the visual arts to enable clients to give expression to their feelings and relationship patterns. In recent years psychodrama and art therapy have become well established specialist counselling approaches, with their own distinctive theoretical models, training courses and professional journals. There has similarly been valuable contact between counselling and literature, primarily through an appreciation that language is the main vehicle for therapeutic work, and that poets, novelists and literary critics have a great deal to say about the use of language. Specific literature-based techniques have also been employed in counselling, such as autobiography, journal writing, poetry writing and bibliotherapy.

1.6. Features of Counselling

Counselling takes place when someone who is troubled invites and allows another person to enter into a particular kind of relationship with them. If a person is not ready to extend this invitation, they may be exposed to the best efforts of expert counsellors for long periods of time, but what will happen will not be counselling.

The person seeking counselling invites another person to provide him or her with time and space characterised by the presence of a number of features that are not readily available in everyday life: permission to speak, respect for difference, confidentiality and affirmation.

1.6.1. Permission to Speak

Mental problems aggravate when there is nobody to here the problems of the depressed. While a counsellor permits the patient to speak, he gets an ear to pour out all his sorrows and they are given every encouragement to give voice to aspects of their experience that have previously been silenced, in their own time and their own way, including the expression of feeling and emotion.

1.6.2. Respect for Difference

Counsellors helps the patients to realise their strength and empower the clients to articulate and act on his or her personal values and desires.

1.6.3. Confidentiality

Personal life is a plethora of secrets. While revealing everything to a counsellor, it is important to keep it as secrets. Counsellors are also obliged to keep their clients' secrets.

1.6.4. Affirmation

Counselling creates a relationship between the counsellor and the client with values such as honesty, integrity, care, belief in the worth and value of individual persons, commitment to dialogue and collaboration, reflexivity, the interdependence of persons, a sense of the common good. These are simple principles, but taken together represent an arena for support, reflection and renewal that is distinctive within modern societies. Within this arena, the client and counsellor make use of whatever cultural resources come to hand (conversation, ideas, theories, rituals, altered states of consciousness, problem-solving algorithms, discourses, technologies) to achieve a satisfactory resolution of the initial problem in living that initiated the decision to engage in counselling.

1.7. Psychotherapy

It is a learning process in which you and your therapist work together to discover what events, situations, and relationships in your current life or earlier life are leaving you with uncomfortable feelings or ways of dealing with your world. You work toward acquiring new, effective, helpful ways of understanding your experiences and the events in your life, your responses to them, and the actions you take. In this way your actions will become less automatic and based more on understanding and choice. Your partner, your child or your entire family might participate in the processes of discovery, learning, and change that are characteristic of psychotherapy.

Psychotherapy begins by creating the private and confidential context in which it can do its job. The work involved in psychotherapy depends on your needs and desires. In some cases the work is to uncover experiences of the past that are brought to the surface by current events, situations, and relationships. This allows present circumstances to be understood and dealt with in a different way.

Exploring painful or uncomfortable symptoms such as persistent symptoms of depression, our fearfulness and unwanted habits and thoughts may decrease in intensity and frequency. Psychotherapy looks at the whole human being and at the many complex factors that have contributed to making every person unique. Symptoms such as anxiety or depression, are viewed not just as a problem, but also as a sign that something is hurting inside that some aspect of the person needs attention,

Psychotherapy assumes that there are aspects of our lives of which we are not fully aware. Our thoughts, feelings, behaviours, dreams, and our reactions to people and events are based on hidden assumptions, expectations, and on memories of earlier events. Our lack of awareness, lack of skill and choice, and many of our old wounds limit much of our untapped creative energy. Psychotherapy affords an opportunity to uncover, describe, explore, learn about, and appreciate our perceptions, our hidden assumptions, the ways we have adapted to life - as well as how all these have evolved.

In a changing family atmosphere, couples and families need to be aware of the mounting tensions within themselves. Psychotherapy can facilitate a more effective understanding of the current relationships, along with a fuller understanding of what you and the others may feel, say, and do in those relationships.

Psychotherapy takes place in the context of a solid, trustworthy working relationship between the client and the therapist. It helps create the context, the insight, and under standing, the vision, and the support within which durable growth and desirable change can take place. Psychotherapy is not advice giving, but it can involve giving advice. It empowers the client to come to useful personal understanding, to make clearer choices, and to a more achieve lasting independence,

Awareness and compromising mentality reduce tensions. We feel in better possession of ourselves and more able to make positive and life-affirming decisions. Creative energies no longer need to be spent on keeping old troubles in control, and there is more energy for love, work and play. We can see past or present events and people more clearly, and we may come to know more about who we are independent of other people's definitions. Some have referred to the psychotherapy experience as the awakening of aspects of the inner self which have been hidden. Others may describe psychotherapy as education, problem solving, changing our environment and minds.

Psychotherapy enables you to see beneath the surface and integrate intellectual understanding with your emotional experiences. The confidential psychotherapy sessions encourage your thoughts and emotional experiences to flow freely. In this free-flowing process, a variety of thoughts and feelings emerge; they create a window through which you can understand your inner processes more directly. You and your therapist jointly examine these moment-to-moment experiences in a non-judgmental manner that provides new understanding about your experience of the world. The process gradually becomes a part of your internal experience and goes with you after therapy is completed.

1.7.1. Types of Therapy

Common types of psychotherapy include:

1.7.1.1. Art Therapy

Art therapy is a form of expressive therapy that uses art materials, such as paints, chalk and markers. Art therapy combines traditional psychotherapeutic theories and techniques with an understanding of the psychological aspects of the creative process, especially the affective properties of the different art materials.

1.7.1.2. Behaviour Therapy

Behaviour therapy focuses on changing unwanted or unhealthy behaviours, typically using a system of rewards, reinforcements of positive behaviour and desensitisation. Desensitisation is a process of confronting something that causes anxiety, fear or discomfort and overcoming those responses. If you have a fear of germs that triggers you to excessively wash your hands, for instance, you might be taught techniques to stop your excessive washing.

1.7.1.3 Cognitive Therapy

Cognitive therapy is designed to help you identify and change distorted thought (cognitive) patterns that can lead to feelings and behaviours that are troublesome, self-defeating or self-destructive. It's based on the premise that how you interpret your experiences in life determines the way you feel and behave. If you have depression, for instance, you might see yourself and your experiences in negative ways, which worsens the symptoms of depression. Like behaviour therapy, cognitive therapy focuses on your current problem, rather than addressing underlying or past issues or conflicts. Unlike behaviour therapy, however, your experiences are an important part of the cognitive therapy process.

1.7.1.4. Cognitive-Behaviour Therapy

Cognitive-behaviour therapy combines features of both cognitive and behaviour therapies to identify unhealthy, negative beliefs and behaviours and replace them with healthy, positive ones. It's based on the idea that your own thoughts - not other people or situations - determine how you behave. Even if an unwanted situation doesn't change, you can change the way you think and behave in a positive way.

1.7.1.5. Dialectical Behaviour Therapy

Dialectical behaviour therapy (DBT) is a type of cognitive-behaviour therapy. Its primary objective is to teach behavioural skills to help you tolerate stress, regulate your emotions and improve your relationships with others. It was originally designed for people with borderline personality disorder, who often have suicidal behaviour. But DBT has been adapted for people with other conditions, too, including eating disorders and substance abuse.

1.7.1.6. Exposure Therapy

Exposure therapy is a form of behaviour therapy that deliberately exposes you to the very thing that you find upsetting or disturbing. It's especially useful for people with obsessive-compulsive disorder or post-traumatic stress disorder. Under controlled circumstances, exposure to the event or things that trigger your obsessive thoughts or traumatic reactions can help you learn to cope with them effectively.

1.7.1.7. Interpersonal Therapy

Interpersonal therapy focuses on your current relationships with other people. The goal is to improve your interpersonal skills - how you relate to others, including family, friends and colleagues. You learn how to evaluate the way you interact with others and develop strategies for dealing with relationship and communication problems.

1.7.1.8. Play Therapy

Play therapy is geared mainly for young children at specific developmental levels. It makes use of a variety of techniques, including playing with dolls or toys, painting or other activities. These techniques allow children to more easily express emotions and feelings if they lack the cognitive development to express themselves with words.

1.8. Psychoanalysis

In psychoanalysis, you examine memories, events and feelings from the past to understand current feelings and behaviour. It's based on the theory that childhood events and biological urges create an unconscious mind that drives how you think, feel and behave. In this type of therapy, you explore those unconscious motivations to help make changes to improve your life. You might also do dream analysis and free association - talking about whatever happens to come to mind.

1.8.1. Psychodynamic Psychotherapy

Psychodynamic psychotherapy, based on the theories of psychoanalysis, focuses on increasing your awareness of unconscious thoughts and behaviours, developing new insights into your motivations, and resolving conflicts to live a happier life. It's one of the most common types of psychotherapy. It's less intense than psychoanalysis and is usually done sitting face to face with a therapist. It's also less frequent - usually once a week - and is shorter term, usually a year or less.

Psychodynamic psychotherapy includes a variety of therapeutic techniques, such as exploring your past, confronting your beliefs and actions, offering support, and interpreting your thoughts and behaviour. That process allows you to become aware of and acknowledge the link between a feeling, thought, symptom or behaviour and an unconscious meaning or motivator. With that new understanding, you can modify unwanted behaviour or thoughts.

1.8.2. Psychoeducation

Psychoeducation explores possible treatments, coping strategies and problem-solving skills for your condition. You might learn about resources in your community, such as support groups or housing options. You can also learn about symptoms that might indicate a potential relapse so that you can take steps to get appropriate treatment. Psychoeducation can be especially useful for people with chronic or severe illnesses, such as schizophrenia.

1.8.3. Professions Mitigate Mental Pain

Counselling psychologist is a counsellor who has initial training in psychology, and who uses psychological methods and models in his or her approach. This label explicitly imports the language of science into counselling, by associating it with a specific scientific discipline. There are also several labels that refer to counsellors who work with particular client groups: for example, mental health counsellor, marriage counsellor or student counsellor. The distinctive feature of these practitioners is that they will possess specialist training and expertise in their particular field in addition to a general counselling training.

Hypnosis is used for helping people with emotional or behavioural difficulties can be traced back to the eighteenth century. However, hypnosis has never been accepted as part of the mainstream of psychotherapeutic or counselling thinking. Certainly, the training that most people who call themselves 'hypnotherapists' have had would tend not to be recognised or accepted by the main professional bodies in counselling or psychotherapy. Similarly, healing approaches, which may involve techniques such as meditation, prayer and the use of massage and herbal remedies, have generally been regarded as outside mainstream counselling. The theoretical basis and practical techniques associated with both hypnotherapy and healing do not, currently, fit readily into the ways that most counsellors and psychotherapists think and work, although many counsellors are interested in these perspectives and there have been many attempts to bridge this gap.

1.9. Difference between Counselling and Psychotherapy

"Psychotherapy" and "counselling" are terms that are often used interchangeably. Although they are very similar, there are some subtle differences as well.

Technically speaking, "counsellor" means "advisor". It involves two people working together to solve a problem. It is a term that is used in conjunction with many types of advice giving. For example, financial planning and spiritual guidance are both types of counselling. Just about anyone at all may claim to be a counsellor if they are in the role of giving advice. The term counselling may also properly be used to refer to what occurs in a relationship with a psychotherapist.

In the context of mental health, "counselling" is generally used to denote a relatively brief treatment that is focused most upon behaviour. It often targets a particular symptom or problematic situation and offers suggestions and advice for dealing with it.

"Psychotherapy" on the other hand is generally a longer term treatment which focuses more on gaining insight into chronic physical and emotional problems. It's focus is on the patient's thought processes and way of being in the world rather than specific problems.

Psychotherapy requires more skill than simple counselling. It is conducted by professionals trained to practice psychotherapy such as a psychiatrist, a trained counsellor, social worker or psychologist. While a psychotherapist is qualified to provide counselling, a counsellor may or may not possess the necessary training and skills to provide psychotherapy.

Counselling is provided under a variety of different labels. To employ a metaphor from the world of business, there are a range of competing products that offer the consumer or client more or less the same service. The upmarket version of the product is sold as 'psychotherapy,' which is provided by practitioners who are usually very highly trained specialist professionals, often with a background in medicine. Psychotherapy can be a lengthy process.

Although there is an increasing interest in forms of 'brief' psychotherapy, which may consist of a series of ten or twelve sessions, it is probably fair to say that most psychotherapists would consider it necessary for clients to be in treatment for a year or more for beneficial results to occur. The most expensive and exclusive version of psychotherapy remains classical Freudian psychoanalysis.

There has been considerable debate over the difference between counselling and psychotherapy. Some would claim that a clear distinction can be made between the two, with psychotherapy representing a deeper, more fundamental or involved process of change with more disturbed clients. Others maintain that counsellors and psychotherapists are basically doing the same kind of work, using identical approaches and techniques, but are required to use different titles in response to the demands of the agencies that employ them. For example, traditionally psychotherapy has been the term used in medical settings such as psychiatric units, and counselling the designation for people working in educational settings such as student counselling centres. One significant difference between counselling and psychotherapy is that much counselling is conducted by non-professional volunteer workers, whereas psychotherapy is an exclusively professional occupation. However, both counselling and psychotherapy can be viewed as activities distinct from advice-giving, caring and teaching.

1.9.1. Counselling vs. Psychotherapy

The terms counselling and psychotherapy are used interchangeably by many by suggesting that only psychoanalysts are really psychotherapists - but this view is not common anywhere else. Others use 'psychotherapy' to refer to longer-term work and 'counselling' to refer to shorter term work. The two terms are commonly used interchangeably in the US, with the obvious exception of 'guidance counselling', which is often provided in educational settings and focuses on career and social issues.

1.9.2. Modern Counselling and Psychotherapy

Modern counselling and psychotherapy have benefited

tremendously from the empirical tradition which was given such impetus by Carl Rogers, even though the research agendas of psychology and counselling have diverged greatly over the last half century. Additional work in cognitive psychology, learning theory and behaviour has informed many therapeutic approaches. The richness of the bodies of both empirical and theoretical work which are now available, coupled with the raw complexity of human beings, has led to a profusion of different approaches to the field. By some accounts, the different strands of counselling and psychotherapy now number in the hundreds. Mainstream approaches, however, are much fewer in number, and over time it is likely that many of the less well-grounded schools of thought will fade away, while more new ones will emerge to take their place. While the main approaches continue to develop, and others appear and then fade away, clients are left to choose for themselves what might be best for them. Hopefully the information provided by this site will be of some help in this process.

1.10. Effectiveness of Counselling and Psychotherapy

Despite clear evidence demonstrating the effectiveness of counselling and psychotherapy, pinning down specific reasons for effectiveness or identifying particularly effective approaches remain tricky.

The effectiveness of counselling and psychotherapy overall is relatively unambiguous: counselling does work. For a wide range of types of psychological distress, both subjective client reports and more objective measurements indicate that counselling and psychotherapy are effective, both in the short term and over longer time periods. For certain kinds of psychological distress, such as depression, some evidence also suggests that the benefits of counselling can interact positively with medications such as anti-depressants: in other words, counselling and medication together sometimes offer better results than either counselling or medication on their own.

Overall, no one therapeutic approach stands out as offering better results than any other. At first glance, it might seem that this failure to discriminate between therapeutic approaches in terms of overall effectiveness could be attributed simply to the fact that different people will respond in their own ways to different types of counselling: if clients choose the 'right' or 'wrong' types of therapy only by accident, this might result in particular types offering good results in some areas and bad results in others, with the overall result that no one type of counselling would stand out. But because studies are typically designed to detect and isolate these types of regularities, we know that random choice about therapy type does not, by itself, provide a sufficient explanation of the evidence.

While no one type of therapy stands out in terms of overall effectiveness, however, individual counsellors clearly do. Within given approaches, research shows very significant variation between individual counsellors. Indeed, the evidence suggests that the abilities of individual therapists may be a more significant factor in determining outcome than therapeutic orientation.

1.10.1. Effectiveness on Clients

The effectiveness of counselling depends of the strength of rapport between a counsellor and his client. This match (or mismatch) can strongly influence how the client feels about the process and the relationship and consequently bears on how easy it is for that client to make progress. Virtually all relevant empirical studies agree that clients benefit more when they are committed to working within the therapeutic approach offered in their particular counselling environment - and some studies suggest that client variables such as this account for about 40% of therapeutic change, more than any other factors.

A client who doubts whether a cognitive model adequately represents their experience probably will find less benefit from cognitive or cognitive behavioural therapy, while a client who would like their counsellor to give them a great deal of advice and instruction may not get very much from person-centred counselling. By analogy, while it is probably possible to walk 5 miles in shoes that are either much too big or painfully small or have too much traction or not enough, the right choice of footwear can make it much easier to do so in comfort, enjoying the scenery along the way, and having some energy left at the end. Likewise, many different kinds of shoes will do for such a walk, but some will be a help while others may actually be a hindrance. Some time spent considering the different types of counselling and psychotherapy available before embarking on a therapeutic journey will be time well spent.

1.10.2. Effectiveness on Counsellors

Individual counsellors needn't concern themselves very much with orientation. This line of thought seems to go along with a kind of 'therapeutic relativism' which suggests that everything has its value, and no way of working with a given client is really better than any other. Similarly, one sometimes hears the view expressed that critically evaluating the theoretical differences between approaches is unimportant, and one can just be entirely pragmatic: do what works. Perhaps the most defeatist approach is that there is just no point learning about various therapeutic approaches, given that none has ever demonstrated a clear overall advantage over others.

There is no justification for inferring from the evidence that a specific individual client will be helped just as much by one approach as by any other. We don't yet have the evidence to answer unambiguously the question of what works for which types of clients, but that doesn't relieve the counsellor of the responsibility to consider what will work for his or her specific clients. Moreover, the absence of evidence about overall differences in effectiveness does not imply that there are no differences in how to be effective.

Some theorists and researchers have gone to considerable effort to account for the success of a given approach in terms of what it might accomplish in light of the theoretical model espoused by another. There may be considerable benefits for the client if the counsellor is effective because he or she is getting it 'right' by design, rather than by accident.

It is difficult to see how a counsellor could just do what works without some grasp of the theoretical underpinnings of whatever overall approach or technique he or she might be inclined to employ with a given client. It is preferable for the client if any suggestions from the counsellor that a particular approach might be helpful are made on the basis of some informed view of why it might work: a counsellor's suggestion of a particular way of working should not be made by default, it should be both deliberate and informed. In other words, it may be true that one should 'do what works', but doing that requires some effort to understand and evaluate underlying theory.

1.11. Conclusion

It is not easy to define counselling. In some respects this can be frustrating for people seeking counselling, because it means that there are many situations in which it can be hard for them to know exactly what is on offer when they consult someone who labels himself or herself as a 'counsellor.' On the other hand, the fact that counselling has been, and continues to be, influenced and shaped by so many different traditions and helping approaches gives it a great deal of its vitality and energy.

References

Carl R. Rogers, *Client-Centered Therapy: Its Current Practice, Implications and Theory*, Boston: Houghton Mifflin, 1965.

Feltham, Colin, *What Is Counselling?*, 1995.

Gladding, S. T., *Counseling: A Comprehensive Profession*, Third Edition, 1996.

Kjell Raaheim, Janek Wankowski & John Radford, *Helping Students to Learn: Teaching, Counselling, Research* (rev. 2nd ed.). Buckingham/ Bristol, PA: Society for Research into Higher Education and Open University Press, 1991.

Sue Wheeler & Jan Birtle, *A Handbook for Personal Tutors*, Buckingham/ Bristol, PA: Society for Research into Higher Education and Open University Press, 1993.

Yalom Irving, His book *Love's Executioner and Other Tales of Psychotherapy*, 1989.

2

Traditional Therapeutic Approaches

Mental sanity is the minimum requirement for a person to lead a peaceful life. Mental disorder is not the outcome of this modern world. It is as old as the emergence of human beings. Therapy or treatment is the attempted remediation of a health problem, usually following a diagnosis.

In the context of mental health, therapy has vastly changed over time. Long before the scientific approach to the treatment of mental health prevailed, attempts to discover the underpinnings of the human mind produced a wide range of therapies and theories. For many centuries, the therapeutic approach to the human mind was mostly based on supernatural and religious beliefs.

Mental illness has its traces in the holy books also. But in olden days, this disorder was treated in a sordid way. Even today, the illiterates are considering it as possession of ghosts and they depend on sorcery for its cure. Switching from a commonly violent and medicine-based treatment to a strictly non-violent and observational approach could produce a better outcome for patients. At this point, the history of the counselling therapy had begun to be shaped.

2.1. Traditional Therapies

The travels of a wayward mind can be checked by using traditional therapies. Mental health professionals use a variety of approaches to give people tools to deal with ingrained, troublesome patterns of behaviour and to help them manage symptoms of mental illness. The best therapists will work with you to design a treatment plan that will be most effective for you. This sometimes involves a single method, or it may involve elements of several different methods, often referred to as an "eclectic approach" to therapy.

2.1.1. Behavioural Therapy

If a person is mentally ill, it will directly reflect on his behaviour. Behavioural therapy focuses on behaviour-changing unwanted behaviours through rewards, reinforcements, and desensitisation. Desensitisation, or Exposure Therapy, is a process of confronting something that arouses anxiety, discomfort, or fear and overcoming the unwanted responses. Behavioural therapy often involves the cooperation of others, especially family and close friends, to reinforce a desired behaviour.

2.1.2. Biomedical Treatment

Medication alone, or in combination with psychotherapy, has proven to be an effective treatment for a number of emotional, behavioural, and mental disorders. The kind of medication a psychiatrist prescribes varies with the disorder and the individual being treated.

2.1.3. Cognitive Therapy

The way of thinking of a mental patient is very different. Cognitive therapy aims to identify and correct distorted thinking patterns that can lead to feelings and behaviours that may be troublesome, self-defeating, or even self-destructive. The goal is to replace such thinking with a more balanced view that, in turn, leads to more fulfilling and productive behaviour.

2.1.4. Cognitive Behavioural Therapy (CBT)

Negative thoughts retard mental growth. CBT is an insight-focused therapy that emphasises recognising and changing negative thoughts and maladaptative beliefs. The approach is based on the theoretical rationale that the way people feel and behave is determined by how they perceive and structure their experience. CBT proposes that change comes about by changing the client's thinking about the situation.

CBT is a combination of cognitive and behavioural therapies, and it helps people change negative thought patterns, beliefs, and behaviours so they can manage symptoms and enjoy more productive, less stressful lives. Once the client has converted his/her point of view, the problem-perception switches to a clearer context. Some basic concepts within the CBT schools of thought include: Arbitrary Inferences: It refers to making conclusions without supporting and relevant evidence. This includes "catastrophising," or thinking of the absolute worst scenario and outcomes for most situations.

Selective Abstraction: It consists of forming conclusions based on isolated details of an event (and ignoring other information). Overgeneralisation: It is a process of holding extreme beliefs on the basis of a single incident and applying them inappropriately to dissimilar events or settings. Personalisation is a tendency for individuals to relate external events to themselves, even when there is no basis for making this connection.

Labelling or Mislabelling: It involves portraying one's identity on the basis of imperfections and mistakes made in the past and allowing them to define one's true identity.

2.1.5. Couples Counselling and Family Therapy

Family is everybody's first institute. A person can come out with either good or bad qualities or a combination of both from a family. We all mould our character from our family. If we born in a good family, it will also reflects on our character. So, family therapy and couples counselling is very much important for nurturing valued citizens.

Here, these two similar approaches to therapy involve discussions and problem-solving sessions facilitated by a therapist-sometimes with the couple or entire family group, sometimes with individuals. Such therapy can help couples and family members improve their understanding of, and the way they respond to, one another. This type of therapy can resolve patterns of behaviour that might lead to more severe mental illness.

Family therapy can help educate the individuals about the nature of mental disorders and teach them skills to cope better with the effects of having a family member with a mental illness-such as how to deal with feelings of anger or guilt.

2.1.6. Electroconvulsive Therapy (ECT)

Electric shock or stimulation is a highly controversial technique, which is used for treating some forms of major depression, acute mania, and some forms of schizophrenia. This highly controversial technique uses low voltage electrical stimulation of the brain to treat. This potentially life-saving technique is considered only when other therapies have failed, when a person is seriously medically ill and/or unable to take medication, or when a person is very likely to commit suicide. Substantial improvements in the equipment, dosing guidelines, and anaesthesia have significantly reduced the possibility of side effects.

2.1.7. Group Therapy

Communication and merry making with friends is inevitable for keeping a healthy mind. This is the underlying principle of group therapy. This form of therapy involves groups of usually 4 to 12 people who have similar problems and who meet regularly with a therapist. The therapist uses the emotional interactions of the group's members to help them get relief from distress and possibly modify their behaviour.

2.1.8. Interpersonal Psychotherapy

Social life is an inevitable aspect of human life. Interpersonal Psychotherapy focuses on the patient's current life and relationships within the family, social, and work environments. The goal is to identify and resolve problems with insight, as well as build on strengths.

2.1.9. Light Therapy

The mental health of a person also depends on the natural forces. Seasonal affective disorder (SAD) is a form of depression that appears related to fluctuations in the exposure to natural light. It usually strikes during autumn and often continues through the winter when natural light is reduced. Researchers have found that people who have SAD can be helped with the symptoms of their illness if they spend blocks of time bathed in light from a special full-spectrum light source, called a "light box."

2.1.10. Play Therapy

Lazy mind will be a den for all evils. So, mind should be active all the time. Geared toward young children, play therapy uses a variety of activities-such as painting, puppets, and dioramas-to establish communication with the therapist and resolve problems. Play allows the child to express emotions and problems that would be too difficult to discuss with another person.

2.1.11. Psychodynamic Psychotherapy

Based on the principles of psychoanalysis, this therapy is less intense, tends to occur once or twice a week, and spans a shorter time. It is based on the premise that human behaviour is determined by one's past experiences, genetic factors, and current situation. This approach recognises the significant influence that emotions and unconscious motivation can have on human behaviour.

2.2. Expressive Therapies

2.2.1. Art Therapy

Drawing, painting, and sculpting help many people to reconcile inner conflicts, release deeply repressed emotions, and foster self-awareness, as well as personal growth. Some mental health providers use art therapy as both a diagnostic tool and as a way to help treat disorders such as depression, abuse-related trauma, and schizophrenia. You may be able to find a therapist in your area who has received special training and certification in art therapy.

2.2.2. Dance/Movement Therapy

Dancing or engaging in physical activities liberates a mind from sadness. Some people find that their spirits soar when they let their feet fly. Others-particularly those who prefer more structure or who feel they have "two left feet"-gain the same sense of release and inner peace from the Eastern martial arts. Those who are recovering from physical, sexual, or emotional abuse may find these techniques especially helpful for gaining a sense of ease with their own bodies. The underlying premise to dance/movement therapy is that it can help a person integrate the emotional, physical, and cognitive facets of "self."

2.2.3. Music/Sound Therapy

Many people turn on soothing music to relax or snazzy tunes to help feel upbeat. Music stimulates the body's natural "feel good" chemicals and this stimulation results in improved blood flow, blood pressure, pulse rate, breathing, and posture changes. Music or sound therapy has been used to treat disorders such as stress, grief, depression, schizophrenia, and autism in children, and to diagnose mental health needs.

2.2.4. Healings from Culture

Culture of a nation also provides some healing effects to a mentally sick person. Traditional oriental medicine (such as acupuncture, shiatsu, and reiki), Indian systems of health care (such as Ayurveda and yoga), and Native American healing practices (such as the Sweat Lodge and Talking Circles) all incorporate the beliefs that:

- Wellness is a state of balance between the spiritual, physical, and mental/emotional "selves."
- An imbalance of forces within the body is the cause of illness.
- Herbal/natural remedies, combined with sound nutrition, exercise, and meditation/prayer, will correct this imbalance.

2.2.5. Acupuncture

The Chinese practice of inserting needles into the body at specific points manipulates the body's flow of energy to balance the endocrine system. This manipulation regulates functions such as heart rate, body temperature, and respiration, as well as sleep patterns and emotional changes. Acupuncture has been used in clinics to assist people with substance abuse disorders through detoxification; to relieve stress and anxiety; to treat attention deficit and hyperactivity disorder in children; to reduce symptoms of depression; and to help people with physical ailments.

2.2.6. Ayurveda

Ayrveda is a priceless ancestral for us from our forefathers. We are passing its goodness generation after generation. Ayurvedic medicines are described as the "knowledge of how to live." It incorporates an individualised regimen-such as diet, meditation, herbal preparations, or other techniques-to treat a variety of conditions, including depression, to facilitate lifestyle changes, and to teach people how to release stress and tension through yoga or transcendental meditation.

2.2.7. Yoga/Meditation

Practitioners of this ancient Indian system of health care use breathing exercises, posture, stretches, and meditation to balance the body's energy centers. Yoga is used in combination with other treatment for depression, anxiety, and stress-related disorders.

2.2.8. Cuentos

Based on folktales, this form of therapy is originated in Puerto Rico. The stories used contain healing themes and models of behaviour such as self-transformation and endurance through adversity. Cuentos is used primarily to help Hispanic children recover from depression and other mental health problems related to leaving one's homeland and living in a foreign culture.

2.3. Techniques for Getting Mental Peace

2.3.1. Biofeedback

Tension free life is a dream for all of us. But in this competitive world, it is very difficult to keep a mind free from tensions. In other words, tensions are also an inevitable part of our life. But one should be smart enough to keep his mind free from such tensions. Learning to control muscle tension and "involuntary" body functioning, such as heart rate and skin temperature, can be a path to mastering one's fears. It is used in combination with, or as an alternative to, medication to treat disorders such as anxiety, panic, and phobias. For example, a person can learn to "retrain" his or her breathing habits in stressful situations to induce relaxation and decrease hyperventilation. Some preliminary research indicates it may offer an additional tool for treating schizophrenia and depression.

2.3.2. Metaphors or Visualisation

This process involves going into a state of deep relaxation and creating a mental image of recovery and wellness. Physicians, nurses, and mental health providers occasionally use this approach to treat alcohol and drug addictions, depression, panic disorders, phobias, and stress.

2.3.3. Massage Therapy

Touching has an immense power to alleviate the sorrows in our heart. Likewise, rubbing, kneading, brushing, and tapping a person's muscles can help release tension and pent emotions. It has been used to treat trauma-related depression and stress.

2.3.4. Technology Medicines for Mental Illness

Technology has developed a lot. All will get technical assistance from all corners of life if we are suffering from some mental illness. The boom in electronic tools at home and in the office makes access to mental health information just a telephone call or a "mouse click" away. Technology is also making treatment more widely available in once-isolated areas.

2.3.5. Telemedicine

Plugging into video and computer technology is a relatively new innovation in health care. It allows both consumers and providers in remote or rural areas to gain access to mental health or specialty expertise. Telemedicine can enable consulting providers to speak to and observe patients directly. It also can be used in education and training programs for generalist clinicians.

2.3.6. Telephone Counselling

A telephone call seeking our health can do a lot to empower a weak mind. Active listening skills are a hallmark of telephone counsellors. These also provide information and referral to interested callers. For many people telephone counselling often is a first step to receiving in-depth mental health care. Such counselling from specially trained mental health providers reaches many people who otherwise might not get the help they need.

2.3.7. E-Communication Medicines

Technologies such as internet, bulletin boards, and electronic mail lists provide access directly to consumers and the public on a wide range of information. On-line consumer groups can exchange information, experiences, and views on mental health, treatment systems, alternative medicine, and other related topics.

2.3.8. Radio Psychiatry

Radio psychiatry was first introduced in the United States in 1976. Radio psychiatrists and psychologists provide advice, information, and referrals in response to a variety of mental health questions from callers.

2.4. Methods to Regaining Mental Health

Usual depressions or sadness is not a sign of mental disorder. But when it intensifies and affects a person's behaviour, it should be treated. Health of a person is depends on the health of his mind, body and spirit. An alternative approach to mental health care is one that emphasises the interrelationship between mind, body, and spirit. Although some alternative approaches have a long history, many remain controversial.

2.4.1. Self-help

Self-help groups are an invaluable resource for recovery and for empowerment. It generally refers to groups or meetings that:

— Involve people who have similar needs

— Are facilitated by a consumer, survivor, or other layperson;

— Assist people to deal with a "life-disrupting" event, such as a death, abuse, serious accident, addiction, or diagnosis of a physical, emotional, or mental disability, for oneself or a relative;

— Are operated on an informal, free-of-charge, and non-profit basis;

— Provide support and education; and

— Are voluntary, anonymous, and confidential.

2.4.2. Food Habit

Mental illness in some persons may appear in form of insatiable hunger. Adjusting both diet and nutrition may help some people with mental illnesses manage their symptoms and promote recovery. Eliminating milk and wheat products can reduce the severity of symptoms for some people who have schizophrenia and some children with autism. Similarly, some holistic/natural physicians use herbal treatments, B-complex vitamins, riboflavin, magnesium, and thiamine to treat anxiety, autism, depression, drug-induced psychoses, and hyperactivity.

2.4.3. Taking Counselling from Religious Heads

Religion has an important role for both fall in madness and recover from mental illness. Extreme faith may make a person mentally sick. On the other hand, respect on the religious heads may help them to recover. Some people prefer to seek help for mental health problems from their pastor, rabbi, or priest, rather than from therapists who are not affiliated with a religious community. Counsellors working within traditional faith communities increasingly are recognising the need to incorporate psychotherapy and/or medication, along with prayer and spirituality, to effectively help some people with mental disorders.

2.4.4. Animal Assisted Therapies

Love can not be controlled. We need somebody to share our love, caress and affection. Working with an animal (or animals) under the guidance of a health care professional may benefit some people with mental illness by facilitating positive changes, such as increased empathy and enhanced socialisation skills. Animals can be used as part of group therapy programs to encourage communication and increase the ability to focus. Developing self-esteem and reducing loneliness and anxiety are just some potential benefits of individual-animal therapy.

2.5. Conclusion

Keeping a healthy mind in this stressful world is a difficult task for most of us. Today, life is very competitive and people are unable to face failures. This mostly ends them in the abysmal of despondence. Some may regain their mental health with inner prowess but some need therapeutic methods to cure mental illness. Today, a mentally depressed person will get help from a number of sources. Innovations and inventions in the field of telecommunication also help people to regain their mental health.

References

Cooper, M., "Therapeutic counselling in schools: A review of current research," *Society for Psychotherapy Research UK Chapter Conference*, Ravenscar, 2007.

_______________ , "Counselling in schools: Findings from an in depth, multi-method evaluation," *11th Annual BACP Research Conference*, Nottingham, 2005.

_______________ and Bryce, S., "Young people's attitudes towards a school-based therapeutic counselling service: Willingness to attend, inhibiting factors and facilitating factors,", *36th Annual Meeting of the Society for Psychotherapy Research*, Montreal, 2005.

_______________ ., "Young people's perceptions of helpful aspects of therapy: A pluralistic model of therapeutic change," *Joint Meeting of European and UK Chapters*, Society for Psychotherapy Research, Lausanne, 2005.

_______________ ., "Teachers' attitudes towards counselling in secondary schools," *9th Annual Counselling and Psychotherapy Research Conference*, Leicester, 2003.

Kottler, Jeffrey A., *On Being a Therapist*, 1986.

_______________ ., *The Imperfect Therapist: Learning From Failure in Therapeutic Practice*, 1989.

_______________ *Compassionate Therapy: Working With Difficult Clients*, 1992.

_______________ *Growing a Therapist*, 1995.

_______________ *The Therapist's Workbook*, 1999.

_______________ *Exploring & Treating Acquisitive Desire*, 1999.

_______________ *Doing Good: Passion and Commitment For Helping Others*, 2000.

_______________ *Making Changes Last*, 2001.

_______________ *Bad Therapy: Master Therapists Share Their Worst Failures*, 2002.

_______________ *Their Finest Hour: Master Therapists Share Their Greatest Success Stories*, 2005.

_______________ *The Client Who Changed Me: Stories of Therapist Personal Transformation*, 2005.

_______________ *Advanced Group Leadership*, 1993.

_______________ *Introduction to Therapeutic Counseling*, 2003.

_______________ *Nuts & Bolts of Helping*, 2000.

_______________ *Learning Group Leadership*, 2001.

_______________ *Theories in Counseling and Therapy*, 2002.

_______________ *One Life at a Time: Helping Skills and Interventions*, 2003.

_______________ *The emerging professional counselor: Student dreams to professional realities*, 2005.

_______________ *Understanding Research: Becoming a Competent and Critical Consumer, 2006.*

3

Individual Counselling and Psychotherapy

3.1. Introduction

With new innovations and inventions, life becomes very simple and we are living in a world which is not restricted with unnecessary frontiers. Now, people can contact or meet anybody by sitting in the comfort of their own home. But it doesn't mean that we are leading a tension free life. Contrary, we are heading towards a very stressful life. People face emotional difficulties through their lives and find it beneficial to enter therapy with an experienced clinician who can guide them through a process of understanding and transformation, in a safe and caring environment.

Psychotherapy is an effective treatment for many problems. These can be life changes, aging, becoming a parent, or graduating from college. Some will find it useful to talk with a professional after experiencing the loss of a loved one, or a divorce, or a re-occurring work-related issue. Still others may experience a lowered level of interest in life, a "flat" feeling, or become anxious and find it hard to stay active in their life.

Getting attention personally is very important for alleviating tension in a certain level. Individual psychotherapy involves regularly scheduled talks between the patient and a mental health professional such as a psychiatrist, psychologist, psychiatric social worker, or nurse. The sessions may focus on current or past problems, experiences, thoughts, feelings, or relationships.

For solving mental problems, the therapist should know things happened in the mind of his client. By sharing experiences with a trained empathic person—talking about their world with someone outside it—individuals with schizophrenia may gradually come to understand more about themselves and their problems. They can also learn to sort out the real from the unreal and distorted.

Psychotherapy, as per mental health professionals, is not effective for individuals with schizophrenia. That is probably true of the insight-oriented psychotherapies that are non-directive, and rely on the client to spontaneously identify problems and discuss them. However, supportive, reality-oriented, individual psychotherapy, and cognitive-behavioural approaches that teach coping and problem-solving skills, can be beneficial for outpatients with schizophrenia. However, psychotherapy is not a substitute for antipsychotic medication, and it is most helpful once drug treatment first has relieved a patient's psychotic symptoms.

The effectiveness of individual psychotherapy depends on the uniqueness of both psychotherapist and client. Nevertheless, psychotherapy is a very specific process. Despite the existence of numerous systems of psychotherapy, the process of psychotherapy has several distinct characteristics.

- It is a systematic treatment
- It is aimed at change and growth in a client or elimination of a client's suffering
- It involves a professional relationship

An authentic, open, and trusting relationship between a client and a therapist is crucial for psychotherapy to be successful. While often the process of psychotherapy involves a conversation between a client and a therapist, it is fundamentally different from a conversation between two friends.

3.2. Individual Counselling

Individual counselling can be used for solving a number of problems. It is an effective solution for a specific problem or symptom. It also helps to deviate an unhappy lifepath into the right way. This change may be in their relationship, with love, with work, with spouse or partner, with friends or with family. We offer assistance at both ends of this continuum: from alleviating symptoms to the search for greater personal happiness.

The problem may be an immediate one that can be quickly addressed or, may reflect lifelong emotional patterns and behaviour. For example, people experiencing anxiety and/or depression often want nothing more than to be relieved of these painful experiences. Often however, they find that these are symptoms of emotional issues that have been building up for years and have affected their relationships, achievements and happiness. Talking to another who understands your concerns—who can offer an objective respectful viewpoint—giving you a chance to find support and new solutions is very helpful.

Each individual is important in this world. The counsellors are just passing this information to their clients. While it is inevitable that a proportion of the clients will need a direct therapeutic approach, with others the focus is on transitional problems experienced by most young adults. Frequently academic work will suffer either because of difficulties directly related to study or because of disorganisation sometimes exacerbated by other issues. The Counsellors work with individual clients who have personal conflicts, relationship difficulties, psychological problems or academic concerns through a therapeutic relationship which facilitates personal exploration of the difficulties and takes into account developmental needs and the special needs of particular student groups, for example, mature, international etc.

3.2.1. Individual Oriented Counselling Theory

Every individual has immense potential to attain his/her own goals. Achieving potential requires favourable conditions and that under adverse conditions, individuals may well not grow and develop in the ways that they otherwise could. When individuals are denied acceptance and positive regard from others—or when that positive regard is made conditional upon the individual behaving in particular ways—they may begin to lose touch with what their own experience means for them, and their innate tendency to grow in a direction consistent with that meaning may be stifled.

Individuals may form a self-concept which includes views of themselves. Because of a fundamental need for positive regard from others, it is easier to 'be' this sort of person—and to receive positive regard from others as a result—than it is to 'be' anything else and risk losing that positive regard. Over time, their intrinsic sense of their own identity and their own evaluations of experience and attributions of value may be replaced by creations partly or even entirely due to the pressures felt from other people. That is, the individual displaces personal judgements and meanings with those of others.

Psychological disturbance occurs when the individual's 'self-concept' begins to clash with immediate personal experience—i.e., when the evidence of the individual's own senses or the individual's own judgement clashes with what the self-concept says 'ought' to be the case. Unfortunately, disturbance is apt to continue as long as the individual depends on the conditionally positive judgements of others for their sense of self-worth and as long as the individual relies on a self-concept designed in part to earn those positive judgements. Experiences which challenge the self-concept are apt to be distorted or even denied altogether in order to preserve it.

3.2.2. Theory of Personality

Carl Rogers' theory of personality evolved out of his work as a clinical psychologist and developed as an offshoot of his theory of client-centered (later called person-centered) therapy. He was first and foremost a therapist, with an abiding respect for the dignity of persons and an interest in persons as subjects rather than objects. Rogers approach to the study of persons is phenomenological and idiographic. His view of human behaviour is that it is "exquisitely rational." He opined that the core of man's nature is essentially positive, and he is a "trustworthy organism." These beliefs are reflected in his theory of personality.

Even though Rogers' humanistic conception of personality has both strengths and weaknesses, it is a valuable contribution to the study of persons, recognising agency, free will and the importance of the self.

3.2.2.1. Actualising Tendency

According to Rogers, the human "organism" has an underlying "actualising tendency," which aims to develop all capacities in ways that maintain or enhance the organism and move it toward autonomy. This tendency is directional, constructive and present in all living things. The actualising tendency can be suppressed but can never be destroyed without the destruction of the organism. The concept of the actualising tendency is the only motive force in the theory. It encompasses all motivations; tension, need, or drive reductions; and creative as well as pleasure-seeking tendencies. Only the organism as a whole has this tendency, parts of it (such as the self) do not.

3.2.2.2. Self

The human organism's "phenomenal field" includes all experiences available at a given moment, both conscious and unconscious. As development occurs, a portion of this field becomes differentiated and this becomes the person's "self." The "self" is a central construct in this theory. It develops through interactions with others and involves awareness of being and functioning. The self-concept is "the organised set of characteristics that the individual perceives as peculiar to himself/herself." It is based largely on the social evaluations he/she has experienced.

3.2.2.3. Self-Actualising Tendency

Self-actualising tendency is a distinctly psychological form of the actualising tendency related to this "self." It involves the actualisation of that portion of experience symbolised in the self. It can be seen as a push to experience oneself in a way that is consistent with one's conscious view of what one is. Connected to the development of the self-concept and self-actualisation are secondary needs: the "need for positive regard from others" and "the need for positive self-regard", an internalised version of the previous. These lead to the favouring of behaviour that is consistent with the person's self-concept.

3.2.2.4. Value Centric Life

When significant others in the person's world provide positive regard that is conditional, rather than unconditional, the person introjects the desired values, making them his/her own, and acquires "conditions of worth." The self-concept then becomes based on these standards of value rather than on organismic evaluation. These conditions of worth disturb the "organismic valuing process," which is a fluid, ongoing process whereby experiences are accurately symbolised and valued according to optimal enhancement of the organism and self. The need for positive self-regard leads to a selective perception of experience in terms of the conditions of worth that now exist. Those experiences in accordance with these conditions are perceived and symbolised accurately in awareness, while those that are not are distorted or denied into awareness. This leads to an "incongruence" between the self as perceived and the actual experience of the organism, resulting in possible confusion, tension, and maladaptive behaviour. Such estrangement is the common human condition. Experiences can be perceived as threatening without conscious awareness via "subception," a form of discrimination without awareness that can result in anxiety.

3.2.2.5. Person and the Self

An individual may develop optimally and avoid the previously described outcomes if they experience only "unconditional positive regard" and no conditions of worth develop. The needs for positive regard from others and positive self-regard would match organismic evaluation and there would be congruence between self and experience, with full psychological adjustment as a result. This ideal human condition is embodied in the "fully functioning person" who is open to experience able to live existentially, is trusting in his/her own organism, expresses feelings freely, acts independently, is creative and lives a richer life; "the good life."

The good life is a process not a state of being. It is a direction, not a destination. For the vast majority of persons who do not have an optimal childhood there is hope for change and development toward psychological maturity via therapy, in which the aim is to dissolve the conditions of worth, achieve a self congruent with experience and restore the organismic valuing process.

Personality change is certainly possible and is further a necessary part of growth. However, self-acceptance is a prerequisite. Rogers originally failed to recognise the importance of "self." As per him, the "self" was a vague, ambiguous, scientifically meaningless term which had gone out of the psychologist's vocabulary with the departure of the introspectionists. According to Rogers, "self is the organised, consistent, conceptual gestalt composed of perceptions of the characteristics of the "I" or "me" and the perceptions of the relationships of the "I" or "me" to others and to various aspects of life, together with the values attached to these perceptions."

The "ideal self," which denotes the self-concept the individual would most like to possess, but other explicit variations are not offered. Similarly, specific concepts related to identity and identity development are missing, although the self image is certainly revisable and undergoes change over the lifespan. Exactly when the differentiation of phenomenal field into self occurs is also not specified.

Rogers believed that the actualising tendency is the most profound truth about man. He finds strong biological support for this tendency in many varied organisms. Rogers' conception of an active forward thrust is a huge departure from the beliefs of Freud and others who posit an aim for tension reduction, equilibrium, or homeostasis. Rogers notes that sensory deprivation studies support this concept as the absence of external stimuli leads to a flood of internal stimuli, not equilibrium.

While the idea of an actualising tendency makes sense, Rogers never specifies what some of the inherent capacities that maintain and enhance life might be. The inherent potentialities of the actualising tendency can suffer distorted expression when maladjustment occurs, resulting in behaviour destructive to oneself and others. The actualisation and self-actualisation tendencies can be at cross purposes with each other when alienation from the true self occurs, so there is organismic movement in one direction and conscious struggle in another.

Rogers believes society, culturally conditions, rewards and reinforces behaviours that are "perversions of the unitary actualising tendency." Rogers finds the human infant to actually be a model of congruence. He/she is seen as completely genuine and integrated, unified in experience, awareness and communication. Distorted perceptions from conditions of worth cause our departure from this integration.

Congruence between self and experience leads to better personality adjustment and less defensiveness. Self-descriptions move toward ideals after counselling and one would assume the closer a person is to full functioning the smaller the discrepancy would be, statements of ideals may be operational representations of conditions of worth, which are socially imposed.

Human being are capable of evaluating the outer and inner situation, understanding herself in its context, making constructive choices as to the next steps in life, and acting on those choices. While humans behave rationally, Rogers maintains that: "The tragedy for most of us is that our defences keep us from being aware of this rationality so that we are consciously moving in one direction, while organismically we are moving in another."

The human capacity for awareness and the ability to symbolise gives us enormous power, but this awareness is a double-edged phenomenon: undistorted awareness can lead to full functioning and a rich life, while distortions in awareness lead to maladjustment and a multitude of destructive behaviours.

The "maladjusted person" is the polar opposite of the fully functioning individual. The maladjusted individual is defensive, maintains rather than enhances his/her life, lives according to a preconceived plan, feels manipulated rather than free, and is common and conforming rather than creative. The fully functioning person, in contrast, is completely defence-free, open to experience, creative and able to live "the good life". Empirical support for the fully functioning person is somewhat mixed.

Carl Rogers' person-centered therapy may well be his most influential contribution to psychology. Rogers' pervasive interest in therapy is what clearly differentiates him from Maslow, despite some similarities in their ideas. The person-centered approach has had impact on domains outside of therapy such as family life, education, leadership, conflict resolution, politics and community health.

3.3. Person-Centric Psychotherapy

Developed by Carl Rogers in 1940s and 1940s, the Person-Centered Therapy (PCT), or Client-centered therapy is used to help a person achieve personal growth and or come to terms with a specific event or problem they are having. The basic elements of this new way of therapy was to have a more personal relationship with the patient to help the patient reach a state of realisation that they can help themselves. He did this by pushing the patient towards growth, great stress on the immediate situation rather than the past. This way the person is able to use the therapy as a way to reach a better sense of self, rather than living in an irrational world.

PCT is based on the principle of talking therapy and is a non-directive approach. The therapist encourages the patient to express their feelings and does not suggest how the person might wish to change, but by listening and then mirroring back what the patient reveals to them, helps them to explore and understand their feelings for themselves. The patient is then able to decide what kind of changes they would like to make and can achieve personal growth. Although this technique has been criticised by some for its lack of structure and set method it has proved to be a hugely effective and popular treatment. PCT is predominantly used by psychologists and counsellors in psychotherapy.

Rogers affirmed individual personal experience as the basis and standard for living and therapeutic effect. Three attitudinal requirements in an effective therapist, in his view, include empathy with the patient's emotions and perspective, genuineness, and unconditional positive regard for the patient. Both active and passive aspects of empathy in the therapist have been identified. This emphasis contrasts with the dispassionate position which may be intended in other therapies.

Living in the present rather than the past or future, with organismic trust, naturalistic faith in your own thoughts and the accuracy in your feelings, and a responsible acknowledgment of your freedom, with a view toward participating fully in our world, contributing to other peoples' lives, are hallmarks of Roger's Person-centered therapy.

3.3.1. Humanistic Touch in Person-Centred Therapy

Rogers' theory emphasised the counsellor's creation of a permissive and non-interventionist climate in which the client is free to move at his own pace and in his own direction. Rogers' basic assumptions were that people were essentially trustworthy; that they have a vast potential for understanding themselves and resolving their own problem without direct intervention on their therapist's part: and that they are capable of self-directed growth if they are involved in a therapeutic relationship. From the beginning Rogers emphasised that the attitude, personal characteristics and quality of the therapist were the prime determinants of the successful outcomes of the therapeutic process. He consistently relegated to a secondary position matters such as the therapist's knowledge of theory and techniques.

3.3.2. Actualising Tendency

Just as plants have an innate tendency to grow from a seed towards their full potential, Rogers believed the same to be true of people. This he called the 'actualising tendency'. For human beings, however, it means more than just growth and survival: rather it is the creative fulfillment of the personality and the reduction in, or satisfaction of, physical and psychological needs. This strong drive continues throughout life as we move towards the fulfillment of all that it is possible for us to achieve and become. None of us ever lives long enough to know our full potential.

3.3.3. Organismic Valuing Process

The ability to weigh up and to value experiences positively/negatively is the 'organismic valuing process.' All humanistic psychologists tend to focus on the whole person rather than isolating different processes such as behaviour, thoughts or feelings. If we listen to our 'organismic valuing process' we will know what will help us move towards our potential.

Difficulties can occur in both our abilities to weigh up and to value experiences and also in our efforts to fulfill our creative potential. If a persons overwhelming need for positive regard from others is not met or is conditional upon 'good behaviour' then the person may internalise the values and beliefs proffered by others. Cut off from their own sense of worth and value individuals continuously strive for the unconditional positive regard they feel they need. They fail and a vicious cycle begins. They begin to behave as others perceive them. Thus the person ceases to trust their organismic valuing process and their personal growth is stunted.

3.3.4. Internal Frame of Reference

A person's subjective world consisting of all memories,

sensations, perceptions and meanings that are available to consciousness is sometimes referred to as the 'internal frame of reference.' In order to understand the behaviour of another person it is necessary to get as close as possible to an understanding of their world or to see the world through their eyes. Striving to 'walk in the client's shoes' and moving away from an 'external frame of reference' of judging, advising, preaching or moralising is an important task for the person-centred counsellor.

3.3.5. Distinctive Features of Therapy

The personal qualities of the therapist are more important than degrees or qualifications in person-centered approach. It regards as essential that individuals realise that they can trust their own experiencing and the validity of their own perceptions. Rogers asserted that if certain necessary conditions are present then changes will occur in the client and the process of growth can take place.

3.3.6. Objectives of Therapy

The prime objective of counselling is to release the individual from any constraints or restrictions. If successful, the client is enabled to explore in safety their inner experiences, long denied or distorted, which are inconsistent with their self-concept. There is no final result or end state; rather, a continuing process of change which will hopefully continue after counselling has ended. Such progress towards becoming 'a fully functioning person' would manifest itself in the person being open to experience, having a clear idea of the path to their own fulfillment; being able to trust their ability to know what is good and bad for their own development; accepting themselves for who and what they are and not only on the opinion of others; and accepting responsibility for their own behaviour.

In facilitating the relationship, counsellor's attitudes are considered to be of paramount importance. There are three counsellor attributes which release a growth—promoting climate in which individuals could move forward and become what they are capable of becoming. These are congruence, empathy and unconditional positive regard.

3.3.6.1. Congruence

The counsellor's outward responses match their inner awareness and feelings; that they are genuine, real, open, authentic and transparent. Congruence is not a question of the counsellor blurting out compulsively every passing feeling; rather it is a state of being. Feelings only are to be expressed when they are persistent and of great strength and when communication of them assists the therapeutic process. Endeavouring to be so open the counsellor acts as a role model sending the message that it's ok to feel and communicate feelings. In order to develop and maintain congruence counsellors need to constantly work at being aware of their underlying feelings and also to realise the importance of having supervision and working on their own personal growth.

3.3.6.2. Empathy

Empathy is the process of understanding another person 'as if you were that person but without ever losing the 'as if' quality'. Rogers described it as a way of laying aside our own views and values in order to enter another's world without prejudice. If the 'as if' quality is lost then the process can become one of identification whereby the counsellor is no longer understanding the event from the client's frame of reference but rather from their own experience of a similar event. When clients' experience their counsellors as deeply empathic they are helped to explore their inner selves more profoundly and change is more likely to occur; alienated clients also feel more connected and less isolated.

3.3.6.3. Unconditional Positive Regard

This means that the counsellor offers the person respect, acceptance caring and appreciation regardless of the client's attitude or behaviour. Rogers often used the word 'prizing' to convey the meaning of this condition. This condition is important because it undermines the clients' beliefs that they are only valued if they behave as required by significant others. There is no longer any need for the client to shy away from aspects of his inner self which may be painful or shameful because he learns that it is possible to be truly himself and still be accepted.

3.4. Therapeutic Evaluation of Person-Centred Counselling

The person-centred approach maintains that three core conditions provide a climate conducive to growth and therapeutic change. They contrast starkly with those conditions believed to be responsible for psychological disturbance. The core conditions are:

i) Unconditional positive regard
ii) Empathic understanding
iii) Congruence

Unconditional positive regard means that the counsellor accepts the client unconditionally and non-judgementally. The client is free to explore all thoughts and feelings, positive or negative, without danger of rejection or condemnation. Crucially, the client is free to explore and to express without having to do anything in particular or meet any particular standards of behaviour to 'earn' positive regard from the counsellor.

Empathic understanding means the counsellor accurately understands the client's thoughts, feelings, and meanings from the client's own perspective. When the counsellor perceives what the world is like from the client's point of view, it demonstrates not only that view has value, but also that the client is being accepted. While, congruence means the counsellor is authentic and genuine. The counsellor does not present an aloof professional facade, but is present and transparent to the client. There is no air of authority or hidden knowledge, and the client does not have to speculate about what the counsellor is 'really like.'

These three core conditions are believed to enable the client to develop and grow in their own way—to strengthen and expand their own identity and to become the person that they 'really' are independently of the pressures of others to act or think in particular ways.

Person-centred theory takes these core conditions as both necessary and sufficient for therapeutic movement to occur—i.e., that if these core conditions are provided, then the client will experience therapeutic change. There is nothing essentially unique about the counselling relationship and that in fact healthy relationships with significant others may well manifest the core conditions and thus be therapeutic, although normally in a transitory sort of way, rather than consistently and continually.

The person-centred approach takes clients as their own best authorities. The focus of person-centred therapy is always on the client's own feelings and thoughts, not on those of the therapist—and certainly not on diagnosis or categorisation. The person-centred therapist makes every attempt to foster an environment in which clients can encounter themselves and become more intimate with their own thoughts, feelings and meanings.

3.4.1. Advantages of Person-centred Counselling

— Person-centred counselling deals with the here and now.

— It recognises and values the whole person.

— It encourages people to believe that they have potential, which with the counsellors help may be recognised and developed.

— It fosters greater self-reliance within the person.

— It is a particularly safe model of counselling because it emphasises staying with clients as opposed to getting ahead of them with interpretations, advice or judgements.

— It encourages the self-development of the counsellor.

3.4.2. Drawbacks

— The process of counselling may be quite lengthy.

— It may place too much emphasis on the person of the counsellor and on their ability to provide the necessary conditions for change and growth.

— It may not place enough emphasis on problem solving techniques.

— It has been described as 'too simple'.

— Some critics say that person-centred counselling uses a limited repertoire of techniques, such as attending, listening and reflecting are used.

3.4.3. Critical Analysis of Person-Centred Counselling

Delivering the core conditions is what all good therapists do anyway, before they move on to applying their expertise and doing the real work of 'making clients better' is the frequent criticism of the person-centred approach. This criticism reflects a misunderstanding of the real challenges of consistently manifesting unconditional positive regard, empathic understanding and congruence. This is especially true of congruence: to the extent that some therapeutic techniques deployed in some other traditions depend on the counsellor's willingness to 'hold back,' mentally formulate hypotheses about the client, or conceal their own personal reactions behind a consistent professional face, there is a real challenge in applying these techniques with the openness and honesty which defines congruence. It may also demonstrate something of a reluctance to take seriously the empirical research on counselling effectiveness and the conclusion that the quality of the client-counsellor relationship is a leading predictor of therapeutic effectiveness—although this is somewhat more controversial, since one might argue that providing the core conditions is not the only way to achieve a quality relationship.

Self is the single most important resource the person-centred counsellor brings to the therapeutic relationship. The client will have transparent access to that self—because the counsellor is congruent—but it doesn't tell us anything else about that self. Whether or not that self should be developed in any particular way, or whether that self should acquire any particular background knowledge, seems to me a question which is more often side-stepped than answered within the person-centred tradition.

3.5. Conclusion

Psychology deals with human beings and their psyche. Our wants are unlimited but the resources to satisfy them are scarce. This makes most of us disappointment. We all face emotional difficulties in our life some how or other. In some people, it will be very intensive. Mental health of a person depends on the physical, economical, emotional and environmental health of that person. The eminent psychotherapist Rogers gave importance to individual therapy. But the people and things a depressed person involves also influence his mental health. In other words, it is a psychology of a human science rather than a natural science.

References

Dryden, Windy & Mytton, Jill, *Four Approaches to Counselling & Psychotherapy*, London & New York: Routledge, 1999.

Merry, Tony and Lusty, Bob, *What is Person-Centered Counselling? A Personal and Practical Guide*, Essex: Gale Centre Publications, 1993.

O'Leary, E. and Keane N., "Person-Centered Therapy", in P. Hawkins and I. Nesteros *Perspectives in Psychology*, Athens: Ellinka Grammata, 1997.

Rogers, C.R., *Counselling and Psychotherapy: New Concepts in Practice*, Boston: Houghton Mifflin, 1942.

______________ ., *Client-Centered Therapy: Its Current Practice, Implications and Theory*, Constable, 1965.

4

Interpersonal Psychotherapy

Interpersonal Psychotherapy (IPT) is one of the short term therapies that have been proven to be effective for the treatment of depression. This psychotherapy focuses on the connection between interactions between people and the development of a person's psychiatric symptoms. Short term usually involves up to 20 sessions (usually weekly meetings, 1 hour per session) and maintains a focus on 1-2 key issues that seem to be most closely related to the depression.

Although depression may not be caused by interpersonal events, it usually has an interpersonal component, that is, it affects relationships and roles in those relationships. IPT was developed to address these interpersonal issues. The precise focus of the therapy targets interpersonal events (such as interpersonal disputes/conflicts, interpersonal role transitions, complicated grief that goes beyond the normal bereavement period) that seems to be most important in the onset and/or maintenance of the depression. The first 1-3 session of IPT are devoted to assessment and identification of the specific interpersonal issue(s) that will be the focus of the remainder of the therapy.

IPT may not be effective in all cases, however, several years of careful study has shown that IPT is equally as effective in the short term treatment of depression as anti-depressant medication therapy. IPT can also work well in conjunction with medications. The decision to use IPT and medications for depression is based on a number of factors such as the severity of the depression, past treatment history, and patient preferences. An IPT clinician (such as a psychologist, psychiatrist or social worker) should present treatment options during the assessment phase and discuss the rationale for IPT.

Since depression is a recurrent illness, it is recommended that successful short term treatment be combined with ongoing, maintenance therapy. Maintenance IPT (IPT-M) can be administered once per month following termination of the short term phase. Preliminary results from ongoing studies suggest that IPT-M may prolong time to recurrence of depression.

4.1. IPT in Healing Depression

IPT is using mainly for the healing of depressive illness. Pharmacotherapy has shown clear benefits for the acute and chronic treatment of the major mood syndromes, namely major depressive disorder (MDD), dysthymic disorder, and bipolar disorder. Antidepressant medications work for most patients, and work for as long as those patients continue to take the medications, but all treatments have limits. A significant proportion of medication responders have residual symptoms that predispose to recurrence or relapse of their mood disorders. Other patients do not respond to medications, refuse to take them, or in many areas of the world simply cannot afford them. For all of these patients, psychotherapies may have utility.

The two principal empirically-based psychotherapeutic interventions for mood disorders are cognitive behavioural therapy (CBT) and interpersonal psychotherapy. Both are diagnosis-targeted, time-limited, resent focused treatments that encourage the patient to regain control of mood and functioning. IPT is based on the so-called common factors of psychotherapy: a treatment alliance in which the therapist empathically engages the patient, helps the patient to feel understood, arouses affect, presents a clear rationale and treatment ritual, and yields success experiences.

Depression is a medical illness, rather than the patient's fault or personal defect; moreover, it is a treatable condition. Building on interpersonal theory and psychosocial research on depression, IPT makes a practical link between the patient's mood and disturbing life events that either trigger or follow from the onset of the mood disorder.

Depression often follows a disturbing change in one's interpersonal environment such as the death of a loved one (complicated bereavement), a struggle with a significant other (role dispute), or some other life upheaval: a geographic or career move, the beginning or ending of a marriage or other relationship, or becoming physically ill (a role transition). Once patients become depressed, symptoms of the illness compromise their interpersonal functioning, and bad events follow.

Although these observations seem commonsensical, many depressed patients turn inward, blaming themselves and losing sight of their environment. Whether life events follow or precede mood changes, the patient's task in therapy is to resolve the disturbing life event(s), building social skills and helping to organise his or her life. If the patient can solve the life problem, depressive symptoms should resolve as well. This coupled effect has been borne out in clinical trials demonstrating the efficacy of IPT for major depression.

4.2. Pattern of Treatment

Interpersonal physiotherapy has three phases, beginning, middle and, end. In the first phase, the therapist identifies the target diagnosis (MDD) and the interpersonal context in which it presents. In diagnosing major depression, the therapist follows DSM-IV or ICD-10 criteria and employs severity measures such as the Hamilton Depression Rating Scale (Ham-D) or Beck Depression Inventory (BDI) to reify the problem as an illness rather than the patient's idiosyncratic defect. The therapist also elicits an "interpersonal inventory," a review of the patient's patterns in relationships, capacity for intimacy, and particularly an evaluation of current relationships.

In the middle phase of treatment, the therapist uses specific strategies to deal with whichever of the four potential problem areas is the focus. This might involve appropriate mourning in complicated bereavement, resolving an interpersonal struggle in a role dispute, helping a patient to mourn the loss of an old role and assume a new one in a role transition, or decreasing social isolation for interpersonal deficits.

The therapy is likely to address the patient's ability to assert his or her needs and wishes in interpersonal encounters, to validate the patient's anger as a normal interpersonal signal and to encourage its efficient expression, and to encourage taking appropriate social risks.

Since IPT has also demonstrated efficacy as a maintenance treatment for recurrent MDD, and since patients who have had multiple episodes are very likely to have more, therapist and patient may decide to end acute treatment as scheduled and then to recontract for ongoing treatment, perhaps of less intensive dosage: e.g., monthly rather than weekly sessions. The IPT therapist's stance is relaxed and supportive. The goal is to be the patient's ally. The acute time limit pressures the patient to take action. No formal homework is assigned, but the goal of solving the focal interpersonal problem area provides an overall task.

The scheduling of sessions once weekly accentuates that the emphasis is on the patient's real life, not the office. In sessions therapist and patient review the past week's events. When the patient succeeds in an interpersonal situation, the therapist acts as a cheerleader, reinforcing healthy interpersonal skills. When the outcome is adverse, the therapist offers sympathy, helps the patient to analyse what went wrong in the situation, brainstorms new interpersonal options, and role plays them with the patient in rehearsal for real life. The patient then tests them out. Given this emphasis on interpersonal interaction, it is not surprising that depressed patients learn new interpersonal skills from IPT that they have not seen with pharmacotherapy.

4.3. Area of Concern

Initially, the role of IPT was to wipe off adult depression but now, it is used as an effective method to treat depression in adolescents, the elderly, and people with Human Immunodeficiency Virus (HIV) infection. There is an IPT conjoint (couple) therapy for people whose marital disputes contribute to depressive episodes. IPT has also been modified for the treatment of a number of disorders, including substance abuse; bulimia and anorexia nervosa; bipolar disorder; and dysthymia. Research is underway to determine the efficacy of IPT in the treatment of patients with panic disorder or borderline personality disorder; depressed caregivers of patients with traumatic brain injuries; depressed pregnant women; and people suffering from protracted bereavement.

IPT and psychodynamic therapy is derived from psychoanalysis, which deals with the unconscious and childhood experiences. Symptoms and personal difficulties are regarded as arising from deep, unresolved personality or character problems. Psychodynamic psychotherapy is a long-term method of treatment, with in-depth exploration of past family relationships as they were perceived during the client's infancy, childhood, and adolescence.

IPT is a useful method for treating seven types of disorders such as: a focus on clients' emotions; an exploration of clients' resistance to treatment; discussion of patterns in clients' relationships and experiences; taking a detailed past history; an emphasis on clients' current interpersonal experiences; exploration of the therapist/client relationship; and the identification of clients' wishes and fantasies. IPT is, however, distinctive for its brevity and its treatment focus. It emphasises the ways in which a person's current relationships and social context cause or maintain symptoms rather than exploring the deep-seated sources of the symptoms. Its goals are rapid symptom reduction and improved social adjustment. A frequent byproduct of IPT treatment is more satisfying relationships in the present.

IPT is useful for:

i) Diagnosing depression explicitly;

ii) Educating the client about depression, its causes, and the various treatments available for it;

iii) Identifying the interpersonal context of depression as it relates to symptom development; and

iv) Developing strategies for the client to follow in coping with the depression.

The short term character of interpersonal therapy restricts therapists to address only one or two problem areas in the client's current functioning. In the early sessions, the therapist and client determine which areas would be most helpful in reducing the client's symptoms. The remaining sessions are then organised toward resolving these agreed-upon problem areas. This time-limited framework distinguishes IPT from therapies that are open-ended in their exploration.

The targeted approach of IPT has demonstrated rapid improvement for patients with problems ranging from mild situational depression to severe depression with a recent history of suicide attempts. Treatment with IPT is often combined with drug therapy, particularly when the client suffers from such mood disorders as depression, dysthymia, or bipolar disorder.

4.3.1. Safety Measures

The therapists of interpersonal therapy are practicing it by following the working manual alone because of the non-availability of training programmes. It is unclear whether reading the manual alone is sufficient to provide an acceptable standard of care. While interpersonal therapy has been adapted for use with substance abusers, it has not demonstrated its effectiveness with this group of patients. Researchers studying patients addicted to opiates or cocaine found little benefit to incorporating IPT into the standard recovery programmes. These findings suggest that another treatment method that offers greater structure and direction would be more successful with these patients.

4.3.2. Functioning of IPT

Even though IPT was developed for treating only depression, now it is used for many mental disorders. Interpersonal therapists focus on the functional role of depression rather than on its etiology or cause, and they look at the ways in which problematic interactions develop when a person becomes depressed. The IPT framework considers clinical depression as having three components: the development of symptoms, which arise from biological, genetic and/or psychodynamic processes; social interactions with other people, which are learned over the course of one's life; and personality, made up of the more enduring traits and behaviours that may predispose a person to depressive symptoms. IPT intervenes at the levels of symptom formation and social functioning, and does not attempt to alter aspects of the client's personality.

4.3.2.1. Treatment for Chronic Disorders in IPT

By eliminating the current depressive symptoms, interpersonal therapy treats the acute episode of depression by eliminating the current depressive symptoms. This approach requires intervening while the person is in the midst of a depression. The acute phase of treatment typically lasts two to four months with weekly sessions.

Many clients terminate treatment at that point, after their symptoms have subsided. Maintenance treatment (IPT-M) is the second treatment plan and is much less commonly utilised than acute treatment. IPT-M is a longer-term therapy based on the principles of interpersonal therapy but with the aim of preventing or reducing the frequency of further depressive episodes. Some clients choose IPT-M after the acute treatment phase. IPT-M can extend over a period of two to three years, with therapy sessions once a month.

4.3.2.2. Psychoeducation in IPT

IPT assumes that depression occurs in a social and interpersonal context that must be understood for improvement to occur. In the first session, the psychiatric history includes a review of the client's current social functioning and current close relationships, their patterns and their mutual expectations. Changes in relationships prior to the onset of symptoms are clarified, such as the death of a loved one, a child leaving home, or worsening marital conflict.

The psychoeducational nature of IPT involves teaching the client about the nature of depression and the ways that it manifests in his or her life and relationships. In the initial sessions, depressive symptoms are reviewed in detail, and the accurate naming of the problem is essential. The therapist then explains depression and its treatment and may explain to the client that he or she has adopted the "sick role." The concept of the "sick role" is derived from the work of a sociologist named Talcott Parsons, and is based on the notion that illness is not merely a condition but a social role that affects the attitudes and behaviours of the client and those around him or her. Over time, the client comes to see that the sick role has increasingly come to govern his or her social interactions.

4.3.2.3. Detecting the Disorders

With an intention to solve unresolved grief; role transitions; interpersonal role disputes (often marital disputes); and interpersonal deficits (deficiencies), the techniques of IPT were developed. In the early sessions, the interpersonal therapist and the client attempt to determine which of these four problems is most closely associated with the onset of the current depressive episode. Therapy is then organised to help the client deal with the interpersonal difficulties in the primary problem area. The coping strategies that the client is encouraged to discover and employ in daily life are tailored to his or her individual situation.

Unresolved Grief: People express sadness, disturbed sleep, and difficulty functioning in normal bereavement but these usually resolve in two to four months. Unresolved grief in depressed people is usually either delayed grief, which has been postponed and then experienced long after the loss; or distorted grief, in which there is no felt emotion of sadness but there may be nonemotional symptoms, often physical. If unresolved grief is identified as the primary issue, the goals of treatment are to facilitate the mourning process. Successful therapy will help the client re-establish interests and relationships that can begin to fill the void of what has been lost.

Role Disputes: It occurs when the client and at least one other significant person have differing expectations of their relationship. The IPT therapist focuses on these disputes if they seem stalled or repetitious, or offer little hope of improvement. The treatment goals include helping the client identify the nature of the dispute; decide on a plan of action; and begin to modify unsatisfying patterns, reassess expectations of the relationship, or both. The therapist does not direct the client to one particular resolution of difficulties and should not attempt to preserve unworkable relationships.

Role Transitions: Transition of roles in life also brings a lot of tensions in the daily life of a person. These may be such transitions as retirement, a career change, moving, or leaving home. People who are clinically depressed are most likely to experience role changes as losses rather than opportunities. The loss may be obvious, as when a marriage ends, or more subtle, as the loss of freedom people experience after the birth of a child. Therapy is terminated when a client has given up the old role; expressed the accompanying feelings of guilt, anger, and loss; acquired new skills; and developed a new social network around the new role.

Interpersonal Deficits: When the client has a history of inadequate or unsupportive interpersonal relationships, there is a scope for interpersonal deficits. The client may never have established lasting or intimate relationships as an adult, and may experience a sense of inadequacy, lack of self-assertion, and guilt about expressing anger. Generally, clients with a history of extreme social isolation come to therapy with more severe emotional disturbances.

The goal of treatment is to reduce the client's social isolation. Instead of focusing on current relationships, IPT therapy in this area focuses on the client's past relationships; the present relationship with the therapist; and ways to form new relationships.

4.4. Implementing IPT in Exceptional People

4.4.1. IPT in Old Age

Senescence is a period of loneliness. In working with the elderly, IPT sessions may be shorter to allow for decreased energy levels, and dependency issues may be more prominent. In addition, the therapist may work with an elderly client toward tolerating rather than eliminating long-standing role disputes.

4.4.2. IPT among HIV Patients

Patients with HIV and AIDS face anathema from the society. In IPT with HIV-positive clients, particular attention is paid to the clients' unique set of psychosocial stressors: the stigma of the disease; the effects of being gay (if applicable); dealing with family members who may isolate themselves; and coping with the medical consequences of the disease.

4.4.3. Adolescents

People in their adolescent period face a train of problems such as separation from parents; the client's authority in relationship to parents; the development of new interpersonal relationships; first experiences of the death of a relative or friend; peer pressure; and single-parent families. Adolescents are seen weekly for 12 weeks with once-weekly additional phone contact between therapist and client for the first four weeks of treatment. The parents are interviewed in the initial session to get a comprehensive history of the adolescent's symptoms, and to educate the parents as well as the young person about depression and possible treatments, including a discussion of the need for medication.

The therapist refrains from giving advice when working with adolescents, and will primarily use supportive listening, while assessing the client for evidence of suicidal thoughts or problems with school attendance. So far, research does not support the efficacy of antidepressant medication in treating adolescents, though most clinicians will give some younger clients a trial of medication if it appears to offer relief.

4.4.4. IPT in Substance Abuse Disorders

Young age is prone to many unhealthy activities such as the use of drugs and narcotic substances. While IPT has not yet demonstrated its efficacy in the field of substance abuse recovery, a version of IPT has been developed for use with substance abusers. The two goals are to help the client stop or cut down on drug use; and to help the client develop better strategies for dealing with the social and interpersonal consequences of drug use. To meet these goals, the client must accept the need to stop; take steps to manage impulsiveness; and recognise the social contexts of drug purchase and use. Relapse is viewed as the rule rather than the exception in treating substance abuse disorders, and the therapist avoids treating the client in a punitive or disapproving manner when it occurs. Instead, the therapist reminds the client of the fact that staying away from drugs is the client's decision.

4.4.5. Treating Eating Disorders

Too much eating is a disorder and IPT has a solution for this problem also. The IPT therapist does not focus directly on the symptoms of the disorder, but rather, allows for identification of problem areas that have contributed to the emergence of the disorder over time. IPT appears to be useful in treating clients with bulimia whose symptoms are maintained by interpersonal issues, including social anxiety; sensitivity to conflict and rejection; and difficulty managing negative emotions.

IPT is helpful in bringing the problems underlying the bingeing and purging to the surface, such as conflict avoidance; difficulties with role expectations; confusion regarding needs for closeness and distance; and deficiencies in solving social problems. IPT also helps people with bulimia to regulate the emotional states that maintain the bulimic behaviour.

There is a connection between interpersonal and family dysfunction and the development of anorexia nervosa. Therapists disagree as to whether interpersonal dysfunction causes or is caused by anorexia. IPT has been helpful because it is not concerned with the origin but rather seeks to improve the client's interpersonal functioning and thereby decreasing symptoms. IPT's four categories of grief, interpersonal disputes, interpersonal deficits, and role transitions correspond to the core issues of clients with anorexia. Social phobia is another disorder that responds well to IPT.

4.5. Care After IPT

Once the balance of the mind has lost, it takes time to come back. There are a lot of things should be continued even if the therapy is over. Interpersonal therapy as a maintenance approach (IPT-M) could be viewed as aftercare for clients suffering from depression. It is designed as a preventive measure by focusing on the period after the acute depression has passed.

Typically, once the client is in remission and is symptom-free, he or she takes on more responsibilities and has increased social contact. These changes can lead to increased stress and greater vulnerability to another episode of depression. IPT-M enables clients to reduce the stresses associated with remission and thereby lower the risk of recurrence. The goal of maintenance therapy is to keep the client at his or her current level of functioning. Research has shown that for clients with a history of recurrent depression, total prevention is unlikely, but that maintenance therapy may delay a recurrence.

Long-term maintenance psychotherapy by itself is not recommended unless there are such reasons as pregnancy or severe side effects that prevent the client from being treated with medication. IPT-M does, however, seem to be particularly helpful with certain groups of patients, either alone or in combination with medication. Women appear to benefit, due to the importance of social environment and social relations in female gender roles; the effects of the menstrual cycle on symptoms; and complications related to victimisation by rape, incest, or battering. IPT is also useful for elderly clients who can't take antidepressants due to intolerable side effects or such medical conditions as autoimmune disorders, cardiovascular disorders, diabetes, or other general medical conditions.

4.6. Conclusion

Interpersonal psychotherapy is a relatively young psychotherapy targeted to particular psychiatric diagnoses. Like other psychotherapies, its characteristics are well defined and its efficacy is well understood. Nonetheless, far more remains unknown about its indications for various conditions, its optimal dosing, its combination with pharmacotherapy, its utility in different formats, and so forth. Although one of the best studied interventions in outcome research, particularly for mood disorders, IPT is only now spreading into clinical practice. It is a fairly simple treatment for already experienced psychotherapists to learn, but its effectiveness in the hands of less trained therapists is moot. Thus the spread of this still relatively "pure" treatment carries both opportunities and dangers.

References

Klerman, Gerald L., and others, *Interpersonal Psychotherapy of Depression*, New York: Basic Books, Inc., 1984.

______________ ., and Myrna M. Weissman, Ph.D., eds., *New Applications of Interpersonal Psychotherapy*, Washington, DC: American Psychiatric Press, Inc., 1993.

5

Group Psychotherapy

5.1. Introduction

Loneliness and isolation makes mad even a healthy mind. Human beings are social animals. Mingling, making friends, chatting liberate human minds and these will help people to keep happy. Here is the importance of group psychotherapy. It is a special form of therapy in which a small number of people meet together under the guidance of a professionally trained therapist to help themselves and one another. The therapy has been widely used and has been a standard treatment option for over 50 years.

Everybody creates group environments, either through their families, schools, organised activities, or work. These are the environments in which we grow and develop as human beings. Group psychotherapy is no different. It provides a place where you come together with others to share problems or concerns, to better understand your own situation, and to learn from and with each other.

Group therapy helps people learn about themselves and improve their interpersonal relationships. It addresses feelings of isolation, depression or anxiety. And it helps people make significant changes so they feel better about the quality of their lives. Additionally, group therapists can apply the principles of group to other settings and situations such as businesses, schools and community organisations.

Group therapy has been shown to be as effective and sometimes even more effective. In cases of medical illness, there is substantial evidence that this form of therapy helps people cope better with their illness, enhances the quality of their lives and, in some cases, such as breast cancer, has even been shown to help people live longer.

5.2. Methods to Conduct Group Therapy

Group therapy is indicated for clients with manifest interpersonal difficulties and interpersonal pathology; individuals who lack self-awareness in the interpersonal realm or who manifest ego-syntonic character pathology; clients who are action-oriented; clients who will benefit from the affective stimulation and interaction that group therapy generally provides; and clients who need either to dilute an overly intense and dependent therapeutic relationship or to intensify an arid, sterile therapeutic relationship who will benefit from the presence of peers to support and challenge them.

Many clients may benefit from group psychotherapy even if they do not identify primary interpersonal difficulties, if the interpersonal underpinnings of their psychological difficulties can be identified and articulated in the pre-group assessment and preparation sessions. People who suffers difficulties with interpersonal relationships, problems facing children and adolescents, aging, medical illness, depression and anxiety, loss, trauma, lifestyle issues within a traditional culture, personality disorders, addictive disorders, etc.

Group therapy session is a collaborative effort in which the therapist assumes clinical responsibility for the group and its members. In a typical session members work to express their own problems, feelings, ideas and reactions as freely and honestly as possible. Such exploration gives the group the important information needed to understand and help one another. Members learn not only to understand themselves and their own issues but also become "therapeutic helpers" for other members.

Those who need help are selected by a group therapist. In meetings, people are encouraged to talk with each other in a spontaneous and honest fashion. A professionally trained therapist, who provides productive examination of the issues or concerns affecting the individuals and the group, guides the discussion.

Every group is not alike. There are a variety of styles that different groups use. For instance, some focus more on interpersonal development, where much of the learning actually comes from the interaction between members. Others address thoughts and behaviours, where the emphasis is on learning how to control negative thoughts, address phobias or relieve anxiety-inducing situations.

While undergoing in group therapy, some people may need individual therapy. Sometimes group therapy is used as the main or only treatment approach. Sometimes it's used along with individual therapy. Often people find that working simultaneously in both group and individual therapy stimulates growth in mutually complementary ways. And clients may see two different therapists for individual and group therapies. In such cases, it's generally considered important for the two therapists to communicate with each other periodically for the client's benefit. Ask your therapist about the type of therapy that will best meet your needs.

5.3. Significance of Group Therapy

Under group therapy, professionals help their clients to improve interpersonal relationships. Group psychotherapy also provides a support network for specific problems or challenges. The psychotherapy group is different from support and self-help groups in that it not only helps people cope with their problems, but also provides for change and growth. Support groups, which are generally led by professionals, help people cope with difficult situations at various times but are usually geared toward alleviating symptoms. Self-help groups usually focus on a particular shared symptom or situation and are usually not led by a trained therapist.

Group therapy provides opportunities to learn with and from other people, to understand one's own patterns of thought and behaviour and those of others, and to perceive how group members react to one another. We live and interact with people every day and often there are things that other people are experiencing or grappling with that can be beneficial to share with others. In group therapy, you learn that perhaps you're not as different as you think or that you're not alone. You'll meet and interact with people, and the whole group learns to work on shared problems - one of the most beneficial aspects. The more you involve yourself in the group, the more you get out of it.

5.3.1. Participants in Group Therapy

Those who are unable to keep a healthy relationship in interpersonal interactions need group therapy. It helps to deal with specific problems such as depression, anxiety, serious medical illness, loss, addictive disorders or behavioural problems. With adolescents, for example, group therapy teaches socialisation skills needed to help function in environments outside the home.

The clients in a group may hesitate to divulge everything even in front of therapist in the beginning. But later they develop feelings of interest and trust. Most clients find that group therapy provides a great deal of relief because it allows them a chance to talk with others who are experiencing similar problems - in a private, confidential setting. Many people who have experienced group therapy believe that working together with others is helpful and they feel better by participating in this form of therapy.

5.3.2. Modus Operandi in a Group

The most important factor in a group is, everyone and no-one is a therapist. In a group, analytic understanding the group is the therapist, which means that group analysis is a form of psychotherapy "by the group, of the group, including its conductor." The primary psychological unit is the group, the primary biological unit is the individual. The process of existing is a process of communication in different, significant groups.

Communication is the foundation stone of the existence of human beings. In a group analytic understanding, the individual is seen as a nodal point in a network of group relations. Psychopathology of the individual expresses a blockage in the communication within significant groups. Only through analysis of the conflictual group relations, this disturbance in the communication process, called psychopathology, can be understood. In a process of free-floating communication, analysing is the task of the group, thus interpretation is not the privilege of the analyst.

The group creates meaning through analysis. Under the specific conditions of a group analytic setting which follows well-defined rules, the group analytic attitude - slowly adopted by all group members - promotes the development of an intermediate space with clear boundaries, in which the group members - including the conductor - develop the ability to communicate and listen to each other in a non-judgemental, free-floating, non-directive and non-manipulative way. In this free-floating communication which provides a maximum of free speech, the unconscious relationship in the network of the group becomes the object of communication and analysis. Conflicts which develop in this dynamic network of group relations can then be understood as figures on the background of the unconscious transference and counter-transference processes. Transference and counter-transference form the link to the outside world. Each patient brings his or her world into the group. Communication becomes the aim in such a free-floating process. In learning to communicate, the group can be compared with a child learning to speak.

5.3.3. Cultivation of Free-Floating Communication Skills

Group analytic attitude describes the technique which opens a space for the group members to reach access to the unconscious process within the group and between groups. Group analysts are not able to deal better with day-to-day conflicts, but they have learned a very specific way of relating within a well-defined group analytic situation which opens the way to the understanding of unconscious conflicts, the social unconscious of the group. Identity is a process which develops through interaction in which the reciprocity of recognition becomes the basic exchange in communication. Individuality develops through the deviation from expectations and norms of these significant communicating groups. With this group analytic attitude the group conductor deviates from the regressive need of the group for a leader.

The group analyst has to accept the unconscious fantasy of the group which puts the therapist in the position of a premordial leader image, one who is omnipotent, and the group expects magical help from him. But instead of fulfilling this regressive need, the conductor uses it in the best interest of the group, which means that he has to change from a leader of the group to a leader in the group, replacing thereby in turn the leader's authority by that of the group. The essential role of group analysis is to replace submission by co-operation on equal terms between equals. By working through this regressive need of a fusion with an omnipotent leader, the group develops the ability to communicate between equals.

5.3.4. Role of Group Therapy

Group therapy reinforces each other's normal reactions and wears down and correct each other's neurotic reactions. To belong to a significant group and to be recognised by the group is a therapeutic force in itself, but it becomes very soon a resistance and a dangerous dynamic within and between groups. This is why in group analytic groups the conductor is through this group analytic attitude the stranger from the beginning. The frustration of dependency needs provokes very powerful emotional reactions. The need to belong to a unified group, makes differences within the group unconscious, the so-called social unconscious of the group. Through the process of a free-floating association within the group, mainly established by the group analytic attitude of the conductor and the basic rule, that every spontaneous thought should be shared, an exchange between different views and experiences can start. This differentiation process goes along with a very painful and slow process of accepting the otherness of the other.

5.3.5. Mirroring

In a free-floating communication, the group members learn to tolerate the ambiguity of communication, which means to understand that each group member tells more than what he or she says. This is one of the preconditions for being able to use other group members as mirrors. Like mirrors allow us to see ourselves from behind, understand of the mirrored meaning of what a group member has said, allows the access to the unconscious meaning of what has been told.

For the process of differentiation, the groups make use of mirroring. Mirroring combines empathy in the other and the notion of being different from the other in one emotional reaction to the perception of the otherness of the other. Through mirroring, similarities and differences between group members are sorted out.

5.3.6. Factors Retarding Effectiveness of Group Therapy

The term anti or negative implies a movement against something contrary to the term "pro" or "positive". In group analytic psychotherapy we have to find ways to protect the group analytic attitude, which helps the group and the acting out member to understand the creative potential of what is being staged. There is not polarity: anti- and pro-group forces, but there is one developmental process in which the survival of destructive attacks and the working through of destructive fantasies sets in motion a process of differentiation between self and object.

It is not a matter of transforming a destructive attack into something creative, but to understand the creative potential of destructive fantasies, which is to transform the object still under omnipotent control into the perception of an external subject in its own rights. If we are able to survive destructive attacks and to put into words our own destructive fantasies, we create a mature inter-subjective space in which all group members are perceived as externals and thus as subjects with their own rights and needs. A transitional space for creativity and love develops between group members. In this sense, destruction comes before desire.

5.4. Therapeutic Relationship in Group

The success of individual group members is intimately linked to the overall health of the group-as-a-whole. Indeed, a sizable portion of the clinical and empirical literature delineates therapeutic factors and mechanisms that have been linked with healthy well-functioning therapy groups. Mechanisms of action are interventions or therapeutic processes that are considered to be causal agents that mediate client improvement. These mechanisms take many forms, including experiential, behavioural and cognitive interventions, as well as processes central to the treatment itself, such as the therapeutic relationship.

Cohesion is the best definition of the therapeutic relationship in group. The therapeutic relationship is the ubiquitous mechanism of action that operates across all therapies. It appears as important, if not more important, in explaining client improvement than the specific theoretical orientation practiced by the therapist.

Cohesion defines the therapeutic relationship in group as comprising multiple alliances that can be observed from three structural perspectives-intra-personal, intra-group and interpersonal. Intrapersonal cohesion interventions focus on members' sense of belonging, acceptance, commitment and allegiance to their group and have been directly related to client improvement.

A critical and unique therapeutic mechanism of change in small group treatment relates to the interpersonal environment, often referred to as the social microcosm created when the leader and members join together in a therapeutic collective. In addition to the therapist's clinical sense, empirical assessment tools provide a structured approach to "taking the pulse" of the group interpersonal climate to ascertain what may be obstructing or facilitating interpersonal processes at a group level. Leaders play a pivotal role in modelling and shaping this interpersonal environment and are advised to pay careful attention to these particular mechanisms of change. It is particularly wise to focus upon the relational bond, working relationship/therapeutic alliance and negative factors. Attention to these elements underscores the possibility that ruptures in the leader-member relationship may occur which can impede the work of therapy for a member or at times for the group as a whole, and even lead to the premature termination of members. Therapeutic interventions intentionally targeting different structural units of the group are encouraged as the therapist creates and/or maintains specific mechanisms of change.

5.4.1. Group Therapy in Dropout Clients

In the process of group therapy, some clients may discontinue it because of various reasons. Therapists can also learn about inclusion and exclusion criteria from the study of clients who have dropped out of group therapy or terminated prematurely. The phenomenon of dropouts is potentially very disruptive in group therapy and generally there is little positive to extract from a dropout experience. Dropouts generally do not benefit personally from group therapy, and may negatively impact their group. They stimulate poor morale and may produce a negative contagion regarding the ineffectiveness of the group.

Individuals who repeatedly engage the group in issues related to their commitment and participation may generate an unhelpful preoccupation and then disappoint and frustrate the group with their departure. Group therapists are advised to consider the risk of early dropout of clients who demonstrate poor psychological mindedness; little self-reflection; poor motivation; high degrees of defensiveness, denial and guardedness; and who elicit angry and negative reactions from others. The therapist's direct experience with such clients in the assessment phase may provide important interpersonal data if it can be harvested by recognition and working through with the client. If not, the hazard is likely that the group will reconfirm for these clients their fundamental negative view of themselves in relationship to the world and reinforce their difficulties rather than create an opportunity for growth or repair.

Group therapy is a difficult treatment for many individuals to undertake as their first treatment. Individuals who have had a prior successful course of therapy or are in concurrent individual therapy will likely do better in group psychotherapy than clients for whom the group is their first psychotherapy experience.

5.4.2. Pre-Group Training

Pre-group preparation can be profoundly beneficial for prospective members and, consequently, for the group as a whole. While there is strong agreement emerging from both expert consensus and research findings that all therapy groups profit from preparation of its members, discrepancy exists regarding how much preparation is ideal, and in what specific ways the group and its members profit from its application. It is well recognised in all aspects of health care delivery that interventions that increase client compliance with treatment recommendations will increase the success rates of treatment. Since all forms of group treatment, regardless of duration, setting or theoretical model report benefits from group preparation, it is useful to identify the common factors that contribute to this effect.

Pre-group preparation represents one aspect of a trans-theoretical approach to psychotherapy, inherent in all forms of group and individual treatment, and research aimed at understanding the change process in psychotherapy. It is widely recognised that a prerequisite for effective treatment consists of three interdependent components of the therapeutic (working) alliance: client and therapist agreement on goals, client and therapist agreement on tasks, and the quality of the bond between client and therapist. Properly conducted pre-group preparation aims to meet all of these prerequisites.

5.4.3. Objectives of the Therapy

5.4.3.1. Formation of a Therapeutic Alliance

The pre-group preparatory meeting not only promotes the initial establishment of the therapeutic alliance between the group leader and prospective group members, it also provides an opportunity for the leader to leverage that relationship into further promoting bonds with the group and other group members. Underscoring scientific support for the robust effectiveness of group therapy is helpful in allaying concerns about group therapy being an economical but second tier therapy. Clarifying expectations of the treatment helps to achieve both patient-therapist agreement and hopefulness.

The shared mutual identification that the group members have with the group leader is the first step in the development of alliances in group. The group leader take advantage of whatever currency he or she earns while establishing an alliance during the preparation phase and parlay that advantage into promoting cohesion in the group and alliances between group members. The alliance forms relatively early in treatment and is predictive of later therapeutic outcome, many sources recommend that the therapist doing the preparation and the therapist leading the group be one and the same.

5.4.3.2. Decrease Anxiety

The main objective of pre-group preparation is to help prospective group members modulate the anxiety that usually accompanies entry into a group, through clarification and demythologising of the group experience. For other members whose anxiety remains out of their awareness, it is important to help them be more conscious of their anxiety, lest they act out these feelings in group in a counter-therapeutic fashion. Because anxiety about entering group is universal and intrinsic, it is helpful to eliminate iatrogenically induced extrinsic anxiety caused by the lack of clarity about goals, tasks, roles, or the direction of the group.

5.4.3.3. Giving Information

Information is geared towards correcting misconceptions and promoting group development by identifying common stumbling blocks, and mitigating unrealistic expectations about group treatment. Key aspects of appropriate group participation, including self-disclosure, interpersonal feedback, confidentiality, extra-group contact and the parameters of termination, are all defined. Requisite norms for effective group therapy can be described, including issues such as attendance, punctuality, attending group under the influence of substances, sub-grouping, and socialising with other group members between group sessions. Special attention needs to be paid to encourage confidentiality in group and the protection of each member's anonymity. The limits of confidentiality in group therapy, relative to individual therapy, must be carefully discussed. Co-members are not legally bound to preserve as confidential the personal information disclosed in the group. Agreement should also be reached regarding the transmission and exchange of information between collaborating therapists in concurrent therapies or for the provision of monitoring medications.

5.4.3.4. Consensus on Objectives

Pre-group preparation provides an opportunity to obtain patients' informed consent and commitment-sometimes written, but usually verbal- for regular attendance, fees, and participation in group for an agreed upon purpose and period of time. The patient's interpersonal patterns can be identified through careful examination of the interactional processes that occur in the here-and-now of the preparation meeting. This not only helps to provide clarity about the patient's goals, it can also prepare the patient experientially for the therapy group's focus on learning though interpersonal interactions. Attempts can be made to predict the patient's experience in group and assess the impact, both positively and negatively, that the prospective member may have on the group.

5.5. Goals of Pre-group Preparation

5.5.1. Impact and Benefit

Pre-group preparation strongly enhances some factors of treatment; there are also indications that other factors will be only mildly impacted, and other factors will demonstrate little or no effect.

5.5.2. Strong Effects

Pre-group preparation is related to more rapid development of group cohesion, less deviation from tasks and goals of group, increased attendance, less attrition, reduced anxiety, better understanding of objectives, roles and behaviour, and increased faith in group as an effective mode of treatment. Evidence also exists suggesting client attraction to the group improves retention.

5.5.3. Mixed Effects

Improved therapy process (interpersonal openness, more self-disclosure), increased cohesion, improved working alliance, and more exploratory behaviour are generally supported by the research evidence. Pre-group preparation appears to be dose related: more preparation sessions with experiential and emotional intensity are more likely to produce a positive impact. Pre-group preparation has been linked to the beneficial effects of early leader-initiated group structure, which in turn has been demonstrated to predict other facilitative group processes and beneficial outcome.

5.5.4. Minimal Effects

The prospective group member will be more likely to stay in the group longer in order to be able to derive benefit from treatment, preparation in itself has not been found to greatly impact outcome greatly. The low relation between preparation and outcome can be explained by a number of factors. Regular participation is a necessary ingredient of a successful outcome but it is insufficient in itself. A distant singular event such as a one or two time preparatory meeting will lose its potency over time. Over the course of treatment, other more influential variables will have greater impact and consequently, a much more persuasive influence on treatment outcome. Even without compelling evidence in all domains, there is clear consensus that the relatively small resource expended in pre-group preparation is certainly worth the investment of time.

5.6. Group Development

Knowledge of group development can help the group therapist discern if member behaviours reflect personal and individual or group developmental issues. Furthermore, an appreciation of how members cope in the face of group developmental issues can aid the therapist in formulating specific interventions that are specific to the developmental stage of the group.

The diversity of developmental models also reflects different types, structures and composition of group therapy approaches. When implementing an outpatient group, the leader establishes certain parameters, including whether the group will be open or closed, time-limited or open-ended, as well as session frequency and duration. Each of these variables influences group development. An open-ended group with a fixed membership will be more likely to manifest cyclical patterns of development than a time-limited, fixed membership group. There is also evidence that groups of different compositions, for example, homogeneous and heterogeneous with regard to member gender, may vary in terms of the durations of each developmental stage.

5.6.1. Preaffiliation

The members will allude to anxiety, ambivalence and uncertainty about the group. Dependence on the leader(s) will be high, alternating with a climate of "flight" from the group situation. Self-disclosure and sharing of therapy goals will eventually emerge, but tentatively. The leader's stance is primarily educative. The leader clarifies the group's purpose and the therapist's role, and offers guidelines for the operation of the group and member participation. Strategically, the leader allows for regulation of interpersonal distance but invites trust, assists the members to identify personal goals, and identifies commonalities between the members. This allows the group interaction to become more structured and predictable.

5.6.2. Power and Control

During this stage, the members begin to engage emotionally. The leader's authority and the safety of the group as a "container" are challenged. Subgroups may emerge as members attempt to establish a status hierarchy. Conflict and the expression of negative feelings of hostility and anger are common. The leader's tasks are to ensure that the group passes safely and successfully through this stage and that a good working alliance begins to emerge amongst the members.

The therapist works to reaffirm the group's purpose and the members' common goals. Ground rules and expectations are reinforced. The therapist encourages group cohesion and interpersonal learning among the members. Strategically, the leader elicits the expression of negative affect and assists members to identify and resolve conflict to demonstrate the embryonic group's potential. Behaviour that is incongruent with the group purpose is confronted if necessary. The leader avoids labelling individuals in terms of specific roles or rigidly identifying with member subgroups.

5.6.3. Intimacy

If the group successively negotiates the conflicts of the preceding stage, member trust, commitment, and willingness to cooperate will increase. Norms for group behaviour become more firmly established. With this structure, the group is characterised by freer communication and feedback and greater cohesion and openness. Leadership functions become shared by the members; the leader is able to assume a more peripheral and less active role. Strategically, the leader's interventions aim to maintain a balance between support and confrontation. The leader's primary tasks are to facilitate the working process regarding feedback, promote insight, and encourage problem-solving in an ongoing manner. A "derailment" of the group process during this stage may suggest that the group members are revisiting a previous developmental issue.

5.6.4. Performing/Differentiation

The group has achieved maturity and functions as a creative system of mutual aid. There is a clearer recognition among the members of the group's strengths and limitations. The process is marked by the open expression and acceptance of interdependence and differences between individuals. The finite nature of a given member's tenure in the group, or the life of the group itself, may be addressed productively by working through ambivalence or defensively through avoidance or the re-emergence of subgroups. The leader's focus is on letting the group run itself. At an intervention level, the leader facilitates member-member empathy and assists the members to acknowledge and amplify individual differences. Interventions addressing both member- and group-level issues can be utilised.

5.6.5. Adjourning/Separation

With an ending in sight, the group experiences an upheaval of sadness, anxiety and anger. The member(s) may experience the ending of therapy as a profound relationship loss, especially if the group has become a source of psychological support. Members may experience a resurgence of presenting problems or symptoms. Defensive efforts at denial or flight will alternate with periods of productive work. Additionally, the members will demonstrate a future orientation and plans for continuing the therapeutic process or maintaining gains. Expressions of both sadness and appreciation are common at this stage. The leader's primary task is to assist with the expression of feelings and attention to unfinished business. The leader facilitates a systematic review and evaluation of the group's progress, encourages planning for the post-group period, and facilitates involvement in the process of saying goodbye. The latter activity is a critical task-unless the termination is properly managed, the gains achieved during treatment can evaporate.

5.7. Ethics in Group Psychotherapy

Group therapy is effective in a certain extend. But it doesn't mean that all individuals benefit from group therapy. In fact, therapeutic groups can directly contribute to adverse outcomes for some clients, including the experience of enduring psychological distress attributable to one's group experience. It is an expectation of professional practice that the group leader commit to provide quality treatment that maximises member benefits while minimising adverse outcomes. This posture reflects an internalised system of values, morals, and behavioural dispositions that contribute to the successful application of ethical standards to the group setting.

Achieving ethical competence not only entails gaining the knowledge of professional guidelines, federal and state statues, and case law related to practice, but also includes the motivation and skills to apply these standards. Clinician knowledge and moral dispositions acquired through social nurturance and professional education are critical to providing ethical care.

Ethical principles can be viewed as the underlying tenets of codes. Ethical principles are aspirational in nature and not enforceable, whereas codes of ethics are mandates for behaviour and require strict professional adherence for their memberships. Therapists should discuss with potential group members the problem of protecting clients' confidentiality from one another, since confidentiality in group settings can be neither guaranteed nor enforced in most states. Group leaders must recognise that confidentiality is an ethically based concept which often has little or no legal basis in group therapy. Although some states do provide privilege to co-patients regarding confidentiality, as in Illinois, most states do not.

A common method of providing informed consent for group members is to have members complete a group confidentiality agreement explaining that co-members have no confidentiality privilege, and describing ways that members can discuss their own progress toward treatment goals without identifying other members.

Informed consent for group therapy includes a discussion of the potential risks and benefits of group therapy and other treatment options. Additional considerations include group expectations regarding physical touch, punctuality, fees, gifts, and leader self-disclosure. Boundary crossings are defined as behaviours that deviate from the usual verbal behaviour but do not harm the client; boundary violations denote those transgressions that are clearly harmful to or exploitative of the patient. Consistently maintaining boundaries with a commitment to understanding the meanings of behaviours that violate the therapeutic frame are critical; however, rigidly refusing to cross a boundary that may be appropriate and therapeutic in a specific context could also have a deleterious effect on the therapeutic relationship.

5.7.1. Dual Relationships

Duality may arise in group therapy in circumstances when therapists have collegial or supervisory relationships with each other; when group members or leader(s) have outside contact with each other in a social context; or when multiple roles exist between and therapist and client. It has been argued that the profession has a significant blind spot about the danger of dual relationships in group psychotherapy.

5.7.2. Checking Adverse Results

Group therapists often informally monitor group member treatment progress, adjusting group interventions in accordance with group leader perceptions of client progress. Research has shown that treatment progress can be formally tracked to great benefit because clinicians have difficulty making accurate prognostic assessments regarding which client is most likely to experience an adverse outcome. More specifically, not only do clinicians have a difficult time identifying which clients may experience an adverse treatment outcome, but there is substantial evidence in individual therapy that if actual data about client progress is provided to clinicians on a regular basis, a significant reduction in adverse outcomes can be achieved.

Treatment monitoring with the goal of preventing deterioration in treatment and better predicting outcome has also been successfully applied to children and adolescents, confirming the notion that identifying potential adverse outcomes before they actually happen may create an opportunity for therapy realignment.

5.8. Concurrent Therapies

Group therapist aim at proper integration of concurrent form of treatment: individual therapy, pharmacotherapy, or a 12-step group. The principles of integration of modalities is useful in ensuring maximum benefit. Therapy integration increases the scope of clients that can be treated in group therapy and respects client choice and autonomy. Combining treatments however carries potential risks and may be contraindicated if the second modality is redundant and unnecessary, or incompatible with the initial therapy. Concurrent individual therapy may dilute the group therapy intensity by reducing the press group members may have to address important material. Engagement within the group may also be diminished if many group members are participants in an individual therapy.

5.8.1. Individual Therapy

Group and individual therapy are generally of equal effectiveness but achieve their results through different mechanisms and therapist intent. While group psychotherapy tends to emphasise the interpersonal and interactional, individual therapy tends to emphasise the intrapsychic. They may be effectively co-administered. Conjoint therapy refers to situations in which the group and individual therapist are different: in combined therapy one therapist provides both treatments.

Conjoint therapy may increase the therapeutic power of treatment by adding the power of multiple therapeutic settings; maturational opportunities; transference objects; observers and interpreters, generally adding group therapy atop an established individual therapy. Clarity about the reason for adding a second therapy and agreement about the objectives of treatment between the referring therapist, group therapist and client increases the likelihood of successful treatment.

Group therapy may be added to individual therapy to move into the interpersonal and multi-personal from the dyadic and intrapsychic; facilitate interpersonal skill acquisition; or activate the psychotherapy. Individual therapy added to group therapy may help maintain a patient in group therapy who might otherwise terminate the group prematurely, or address psychological issues the group unlocks for the client that require more focused attention. Simply adding a second therapy is unlikely to remedy a resistance to the first therapy and may encourage avoidance of working through.

Conjoint therapy works best when the client provides informed consent for ad lib communication between the group and individual therapist; recognises the importance of working in good faith in both modalities; and accepts the responsibility of bringing clinical material appropriately to each setting. A mutual, respectful collaboration between the individual and group therapist reduces the potential for competitiveness, rivalry, counter-transference or client splitting and projections of idealisation and devaluation to undermine one modality or the other. Mutual respect and open dialogue between both therapists, although time-consuming, increases therapy effectiveness. Failure to communicate between therapists may well undermine both psychotherapies.

In combined group and individual therapy one therapist provides both forms of therapy and hence may have fuller and more immediate access to client information than in conjoint therapy. The group should be homogeneous for this dimension to reduce the potential of stimulating envy and generating unequal status of clients in group therapy. Frequency of meetings in conjoint and combined therapy can be determined mutually and may occur once-weekly for both or weekly only for group therapy with the individual therapy occurring at various frequencies. Ending of therapy can be done simultaneously or sequentially, mindful however that each therapy's ending is fully addressed.

Dealing with client information at the interface of modalities may pose a therapeutic challenge that can be best addressed by underscoring the client's responsibility for bridging between settings. The therapist should operate with maximum discretion and judgment but can offer no guarantee of absolute confidentiality across modalities.

Difficulties in addressing relevant material in one setting or the other is best viewed as an opportunity to understand core difficulties within the client and the feeling of impasse may become an important therapeutic opportunity. Therapists are encouraged to preserve the essence of each treatment modality and explore in detail interface points between the modalities with a view to deepening the work in each. The therapist may encourage the client to address material in the appropriate setting and may ultimately introduce it if therapist efforts to support and facilitate the client addressing the interface through encouragement and gradually increasing the degree of inference in interventions fail. Working through the resistance is generally of greater therapeutic value than merely achieving the self-disclosure.

5.8.2. Pharmacotherapy

A majority of group therapists will have clients in their groups who will require pharmacotherapy, often for treatment of chronic depression, chronic dysthymia and co-morbid personality and depressive difficulties. Often untreated depression is a cause of impasse in psychotherapy and the appropriate use of antidepressant medication may increase the client's access to psychotherapy, creating a level playing field for psychological treatment to ensue. Alternately, group therapy in a post-acute phase of treatment may provide interpersonal and cognitive skills that will improve patient resilience and diminish vulnerability to subsequent relapse.

If the group therapist is the prescriber of medication, logistical difficulties may arise regarding proper monitoring of the antidepressant medication within the group setting alone. For this reason a separate meeting is indicated for monitoring of medication.

5.8.3. Twelve-Step Groups

The broad reach of 12-step groups and their recognised effectiveness in facilitating abstinence from addictions predict the likelihood that clients that have been in 12-step groups or are currently in 12-step groups will also be in leader-led group psychotherapy. In this instance, as there is no other treater, it becomes the responsibility of the group therapist to facilitate the collaboration between the two models of treatment, building atop the 12-step treatment, by addressing the psychological and interpersonal context of addiction in a complementary fashion.

Two important issues distinguish 12-step groups from group psychotherapy: First, feedback or core cross-talk is virtually absent in 12-step groups in contrast with their high value in group psychotherapy. Second, attitudes toward extra-group contact are very different in 12-step groups. Extra-group contact between members and the sponsor/sponsee relationship are of critical importance in contrast to the less permeable boundary issues around extra-group contact in group therapy. Recognising these differences, the group therapist can better prepare a client transitioning into a psychotherapy group from a 12-step group environment, anticipating potential sources of antipathy, confusion or apprehension about the different ways in which these two group formats work. The maintenance of sobriety is a key objective in the treatment of clients with addictions, and the group leader may need to pace the process of exploration so that it is containable by the client, cognisant of client vulnerabilities to relapse.

5.9. Extinction of Group Psychotherapy

The lack of attention leads to the ending or termination phase of psychotherapy. The end phase of an individual's participation in group psychotherapy is typically the capstone of the treatment. While forming and establishing different relationships in the treatment group are crucial and working through conflict is essential, the end stage and the various aspects of the termination process can crystallise individual gains and promote the internalisation of the therapy experience. Hence the ending phase is best not casually dismissed but rather embraced as a time for meaningful work.

The ending process in a group may also stimulate a resurgence of presenting symptoms and/or previous conflicts in the group. Moreover, the ending may stimulate unresolved conflicts related to previous losses and separation. Termination can provide reinforcement for change and growth in the clients as they experiment with new behaviours in dealing with the ending, and have the positive experience of completing a task or phase of life. Termination is also an opportunity for the individual patient to re-examine and rework their relationship with the therapist(s) and group members. In this process of reworking current relationships, the individual member is afforded the opportunity to practice new behaviours and develop tools for her future.

5.9.1. Specialisation of Termination

In group therapy, the ending process and termination must be examined from three perspectives. Individual clients make their own decisions to become involved and depart on their own terms and in their own way. There are those situations where a therapist who functions alone or with a co-therapist must leave the therapy group. Each of these aspects, "time boundary," "individual client behaviour," and "therapist changes" play a role in how termination and the ending process is experienced and worked with therapeutically.

5.9.2. Time Limited Groups

Time limited groups are homogeneous on one or more variables: age, gender, presenting problem, experience of loss, shared life circumstance. In the group a common theme emerges, the resulting group interaction will initiate support, energise confrontation of external and internal conflicts, and promote experimentation with new behaviour in relationship to the problematic issue around which the group is organised. Individual members will come to experience camaraderie, see similarities and differences in coping styles among the members, and bring to the group their typical expectations of leaders/ experts in helping to seek solutions to personal problems.

5.9.3. Endings in Time Limited Groups

There are four levels of focus at the time of ending a time- limited group. One, the group focuses on its own development and the sense of cohesion and group identity which emerges. Leaving therapy after becoming part of a group which is nurturing and supportive may stimulate memories of previous groups which were more or less supportive. Two, the group focuses on individual relationships between members which were supportive and/or conflicted. The leader urges a process of focusing on these interactions and establishing a climate of learning from the experience. Three, the leader engages the group and individuals to process their interactions with the leader. The leader invites the group to process the positive and negative contributions of the leader. In this phase, individuals in the group may rework their typical expectations of authority, leaders and experts, in seeking solutions to personal problems. And four, the leader guides the group to review the respective symptom(s), trauma, or life event which initiated the formation of the group. In this process, members refine or master new coping skills and anticipate how the lessons of therapy can be applied in the future. The leader invites group members to focus upon their relations with one another and with the leader.

Individuals may resolve conflicts and distorted perceptions of one another. Group members learn the benefits of mutuality and shared problem solving. They learn how to work with people who are similar and different from themselves. By focusing on the ending process, the leader helps the individuals to see their own style in coping with change and endings. The goal is to help the individuals apply the process of the group ending to future transitions and endings in their life.

Time limited groups are frequently organised around themes and there is a limited focus on screening for dysfunctional behaviour. Only over time and during the ending process of a time-limited group will the leader(s) and individual members become aware that continued therapy and/or evaluation of personal behaviour is necessary. The leader(s) of time-limited groups should arrange for referral to adjunct professional services for those individuals who need continued professional intervention.

5.9.4. Open - Ended Groups

An open ended group is organised to be a continuously functioning therapy group meeting regularly, typically weekly. All members are expected to attend weekly and announce absences in advance. The therapy group has the related goals of dealing with dysfunctional behaviour and seeking personal growth through interactions within the group. The expectation is that individual members will continue involvement with the therapy until they have reached their individual goals. Individual therapy goals are typically established by the client in collaboration with the therapist and with the group as the therapy process evolves.

Individuals leave the group if the group is open-ended and this process will continue. This interactional process format allows the development of relationships over time which mirrors the formation of relationships in life. The development of cohesion, emergence and resolution of conflict, shared hopes and fears, and departures of all kinds are expected to occur. Departures may be premature, conflicted, sad, joyous, satisfying, with each posing various challenges and opportunities to the therapist and continuing group. This kind of group therapy provides participants with the unique opportunity of mourning the loss of a therapy relationship while still in the company of others experiencing the same loss.

5.9.5. Unanticipated Terminations

This may occur at different stages in the development of a group. The therapist's role is to help the departing individual find alternate treatment formats and leave with dignity, while at the same time assisting the group members to assimilate the experience and to focus on their perceived role in the process of the departure. A premature termination will frequently stimulate the group's first experience with separation/individuation issues. The therapist has the dual responsibilities of helping the individual client continue to make informed decisions for his or her own benefit and also helping to maintain the integrity of the treatment group.

Premature or unanticipated terminations in the middle and ending stages of a therapy group will have different impact and meaning to the group and its individual members. These departures are more likely to include some form of acting out by the individual client in which the personal conflicts of the client are intertwined with the current process of the group. In these instances, the therapist should be alert to the multiple meanings of these departures.

5.9.6. Finishing Therapy with Satisfaction

The patients or clients are undergoing a prescribed treatment for a complete cure of his problems. A therapeutic ending in these instances will include taking time to say good-bye and to disengage from the relationships of the group. The therapist provides a structure to the ending process.

There is a parallel process in the beginning and end: At the start, the individual makes an initial commitment which leads to a long term stay. In the ending process, the individual is invited to set a deadline which permits the group to work through the departure. The reality of the ending is made clear in setting a date. The ending may be set in weeks, months or longer depending upon the individual client and group and the tenure the member has had in the group. The therapist's role is to set the norms which permit the group to learn from the beginning and ending process.

In contrast to premature endings which frequently stimulate negative and mixed feelings, the planned departure will prompt other developmental and interpersonal issues. In the planned ending, re-enactments of positive and negative sibling relationships may emerge. Group members may experience envy with another person's success. Members become more aware of mutual dependency in their relationships. In the successful therapy ending, the therapist is seen less as an iconic figure and is experienced both as a real person and an effective therapist or professional.

The therapist will address various forms of change which may occur. The departing member may report changes in his emotional and affective experience; changes in how he thinks and perceives people; or changes in his behaviour. It is useful for the therapist to remind the client of the problems or issues which initiated the therapy. This process is applied to all in the therapy group since the departure of one member will stimulate comparable issues in all of the individuals. The therapist is also encouraged to focus on the relationships that the individual has formed with current and past group members. This allows for a reworking of those relationships, particularly with those who are currently in the treatment group. Once again, this process will be shared by all of the members. In this regard, it is helpful to remind the group that the departure is a leave taking from the group as a whole and echoes earlier leave takings, but this time with the opportunity to make the ending as full and complete as possible, leaving as little unsaid and undone as is possible.

5.9.7 Impasse in Open Ended Group

The sole purpose of a therapy is to help the clients to regain their conscience. In this treatment environment, an individual may develop a dependent attachment to the group, or her personal conflicts may lead to an avoidance of considering an end to the treatment. In these situations, the therapist has a responsibility to help those individuals who are reluctant to address the issue of termination and the impact this plays in their life and group participation.

5.9.8. End Process

In group therapy, everybody forms a relationship between each other and so leaving them for ever is a painful act. Saying good-bye is a complex process which includes cognitive, affective and interpersonal aspects. The major role for the therapist is to help the group learn from the experience by continuing to focus on the current ending, comparing this leave taking to previous departures in the lives of the individuals and guiding the members to address what they expect to take away from the group experience.

Gift giving, sharing of food, and physical expressions of positive regard through a hug, embrace or handshake are not uncommon. Frequently group members ask about the protocol of gifts or bringing food. The leader attempts to strike a balance, on the one hand normalising the expression of positive feelings and sadness associated with ending, and at the same time offering an intellectual understanding of the process which promotes continued learning and therapeutic gains from the ending. Promoting a warm and engaging good-bye may be an antidote to previously negative or toxic departures and provides a model for future leave takings.

5.9.9. Therapist Departures

The therapy may discontinue due to the departure of therapist, which include training situations, groups led in institutions or agencies, a therapist closing a practice and the illness or death of a therapist.

In training situations in which a co-leader is in a student role with a senior therapist, it is essential that the group know the co-leader's status as well as the time commitment of the trainee. This information sets the frame for the members and allows the individuals and group to work with their perception of the trainee, and the relationship between the co-leaders. Additionally, the set time for the departure introduces the opportunity to deal with the therapist's termination. Similar consideration applies to groups in institutional settings in which a group therapist's departure may be imposed due to logistical and practical factors distinct from therapist choice. A therapist who is closing a practice or ending a group has the responsibility to attend to the therapeutic needs of her clients. The therapist should be prepared to process how group members expect to relate to the therapist in the future.

Personal illness or emergency may take a therapist away from an ongoing group. While crisis, illness and emergency by definition cannot be predicted or controlled, it is useful for a therapist to consider and make a plan for how ongoing therapy responsibilities will be maintained. Support staff or others will need to contact clients about the unavailability of the therapist and to provide information about the anticipated return. In extended absences, referral to colleagues and agency resources may be appropriate. In any event, these situations stimulate a variety of responses in group members which range from an experience of traumatic loss to sadness, grief and empathic understanding of the humanity of the therapist.

5.10. Conclusion

Social life and interpersonal relationships are inevitable for every people. Loneliness instigates a restless mind to travel wantonly and it will end in mental disorders. Group therapy is also based on such concept and through this, the therapists help their clients to knit together such values in their life.

References

Agazarian, Y., *Systems-centered therapy for groups*, New York: Guilford Press, 1997.

Bauer, G. P., & Kobos, J. C., *Brief psychotherapy: Short-term psychodynamic intervention*, Northvale, NJ: J, 1987.

Budman, S. H., & Gurman, A. S., *Theory and practice of brief psychotherapy*, New York: Guilford Press, 1988.

Corey, M.S., & Corey, G., *Groups: Process and practice* (5th ed.), Pacific Grove, CA: Brooks/Cole, 1997.

Friedman, W. H., *Referring patients for group psychotherapy: Some guidelines*, Hospital & Community Psychiatry, 1976.

Grunebaum, H. & Kates, W., "Whom to refer for group psychotherapy", *American Journal of Psychiatry*, 1977

Powdermaker, F. & Frank, J. *Group Psychotherapy: Studies in Methodology of Research and Therapy*, Cambridge MA: Harvard University Press, 1953.

Price, J. R., Hescheles, D. R., & Price, A. R. (Eds.), *A guide to starting psychotherapy groups*, San Diego: Academic Press, 1999.

6

Psychoanalysis

6.1. Introduction

Psychoanalysis is "a therapeutic method, originated by Sigmund Freud, for treating mental disorders by investigating the interaction of conscious and unconscious elements in the patient's mind and bringing repressed fears and conflicts into the conscious mind, using techniques such as dream interpretation and free association."

The term psychodynamic means the active forces within the personality that motivate our behaviour, and the inner causes of behaviour. While Freud's was the original psychodynamic theory, the approach includes all those theories based on his ideas, such as those of Jung who did a lot of study on dreams conscious and sub conscious, Adler and Errikson. Freud's psychodynamic theory is psychodynamic, but the psychodynamic theories of Jung aren't psychodynamic. So the two terms aren't synonymous. However, because of their enormous influence, Freuds ideas will be emphasised.

6.2. Principles and Assumptions of Psychoanalytic Theory

Generally, people are guided by unconscious thoughts, wishes, memories and so on. What we're consciously aware of at any one time represents the tip of an iceberg: most of our thoughts and ideas are totally inaccessible at that moment or are totally inaccessible. These unconscious thoughts and ideas can become conscious through the use of special techniques, such as free association, dream interpretation and transference the cornerstones of psychoanalysis.

Mostly we try to forget unpleasant experiences. They may become accessible, locked away from our conscious awareness.

This is a major form of ego defence. Freud singled it out as a special cornerstone 'on which the whole structure of psychoanalysis rests.' It is the most essential part of it. Repression is closely related to resistance, interpretation of which is another key technique used in psychoanalysis.

The sexual instinct or drive is active from birth and develops through a series of five psychosexual stages. The most important of these is phallic stage. During which all children experience the Oedipus complex. In fact, Freud used the German word 'trieb', which translates as 'drive,' rather than instinct, which was meant to imply that experience played a crucial role in determining the 'fate' of sexual energy. Related to infantile sexuality is the general impact of early experiences on later personality.

Plato was the pioneer to discuss unconscious functioning but it was described more clearly and more completely by Sigmund Freud, who modified his theories several times over a period of almost 50 years of attempting to treat patients who suffered with mental problems.

6.2.1 Origin of Psychoanalysis

Sigmund Freud, a neurologist, developed psychoanalysis in Vienna in the 1890s. He was interested in finding an effective treatment for patients with neurotic or hysterical symptoms. Freud got an opportunity to study with Jean-Martin Charcot, the famed neurologist and syphilologist, in the late 1880s in Paris. Charcot had become interested in patients who had symptoms that mimicked general paresis, the psychotic illness that occurs due to tertiary syphilis. Charcot had found that many patients experienced paralyses, pains, coughs, and a variety of other symptoms with no demonstrable physical etiology (cause). Prior to Charcot's work, women were thought to have a wandering uterus. But Freud learned that men could have psychosomatic symptoms as well. As a result of talking with patients, Freud learned that the majority complained of sexual problems, especially coitus interruptus as birth control, which surprised him greatly.

Freud proposed that the unacceptable sexual wishes were repressed into the "System Unconscious" unconscious due to "society's" condemnation of premarital sexual activity, and this repression created anxiety. Freud also discovered what most of us take for granted today: that dreams were symbolic and specific to the dreamer. Often, dreams give clues to unconscious conflicts, and for this reason, Freud referred to dreams as the "royal road to the Unconscious."

The discovery of narcissism in 1915, and the study of paranoia, masochism, and depression in 1917, Freud eventually reorganised his data into what became known as structural theory in a small book called The Ego and the Id in 1923. This new theory, which addressed the cause of neurotic symptoms—phobias, compulsions, obsessions, depressions, and "hysterical" conversions—amongst others, suggested that such problems were created by conflicts among various wishes and guilt, which produced anxiety. To handle the anxiety, the mind forgot or repressed certain conflicting thoughts. In other words, now he felt that anxiety produced repression, not the other way around.

Psychoanalysis faced severe criticisms from all corners. Though it has been thriving as a research tool into childhood development, and has developed into a flexible, effective treatment for certain mental disturbances. In the 1960s, Freud's early thoughts on the childhood development of female sexuality were challenged; this challenge led to the development of a variety of understandings of female sexual development, many of which modified the timing and normality of several of Freud's theories.

Most contemporary North American psychoanalysts employ theories that, while based on those of Sigmund Freud, include many modifications of theory and practice developed since his death in 1939. Masturbation was later added as another "Royal road to the Unconscious." The definitive text, covering the developmental and symbolic elements of masturbation, was prepared by Marcus and Francis in "Masturbation—from Infancy to Senescence."

6.3. Psychoanalysis Theories

6.3.1. Conflict Theory

Emotional symptoms and character traits are complex solutions to intrapsychic conflict. Freud's structural theory dispenses with the concepts of a fixed id, ego and superego, and instead posits unconscious and conscious conflict among wishes (dependent, controlling, sexual, and aggressive), guilt and shame, emotions (especially anxiety and depressive affect), and defensive operations that shut off from consciousness some aspect of the others. Moreover, healthy functioning (adaptive) is also determined, to a great extent, by resolutions of conflict.

A major goal of modern conflict theorist analysts is to attempt to change the balance of conflict through making aspects of the less adaptive solutions (also called compromise formations) conscious so that they can be rethought, and more adaptive solutions found.

6.3.2. Ego Psychology

Freud was the first person who mentioned about ego psychology. The autonomous ego functions include: sensory perception, motor control, symbolic thought, logical thought, speech, abstraction, integration (synthesis), orientation, concentration, judgment about danger, reality testing, adaptive ability, executive decision-making, hygiene, and self-preservation.

Freud noted inhibition as a way the mind may interfere with any of these functions to avoid painful emotions. Hartmann pointed out that there may be delays or deficits in such functions. Frosch described differences in those people who demonstrated damage to their relationship to reality, but who seemed able to test it. Deficits in the capacity to organise thought are sometimes referred to as blocking or loose associations, and are characteristic of the schizophrenias.

Deficits in abstraction ability and self-preservation also suggest psychosis in adults. Deficits in orientation and sensorium are often indicative of a medical illness affecting the brain. Deficits in certain ego functions are routinely found in severely sexually or physically abused children, where powerful affects generated throughout childhood seem to have eroded some functional development.

Kernberg described ego strengths later by including the capacities to control oral, sexual, and destructive impulses; to tolerate painful affects without falling apart; and to prevent the eruption into consciousness of bizarre symbolic fantasy.

Defensive activity, which shuts certain conflictual thoughts, fantasies, and sensations out of consciousness, is also sometimes included here, although defensive operations are different from autonomous functions. Nevertheless, the term "ego defence" has become common. The overall outcome or 'aim' of ego psychology is to empower the ego to cope with the demands of the superego.

6.3.3. Object Relations Theory

This theory was pioneered in the 1940s and 50's by British psychologists Ronald Fairbairn, D.W. Winnicott, Harry Guntrip, and others. It constructs on the foundation that the ego-self exists only in relation to other objects, which may be external or internal. The internal objects are internalised versions of external objects, primarily formed from early interactions with the parents. There are three fundamental "affects" that can exist between the self and the other—attachment, frustration, and rejection. These affects are universal emotional states that are major building blocks of the personality.

Sigmund Freud developed the concept object relation to describe or emphasise that bodily drives satisfy their need through a medium, an object, on a specific locus. The central thesis in Melanie Klein's object relations theory was that objects play a decisive role in the development of a subject and can be either part-objects or whole-objects, i.e. a single organ (a mother's breast) or a whole person (a mother). Consequently both mother or just the mother's breast can be the locus of satisfaction for a drive.

According to traditional psychoanalysis, there are at least two types of drives, the libido, and the death drive. Thus, the objects can be receivers of both love and hate, the affective effects of the libido and the death drive. Another use of part-object vs. whole-object relates to the inability of young children to conceive of an object which can be both 'good' and 'bad.' Because of this inability, children view objects as either all-good or all-bad, thus only seeing a part of that object instead of the object's whole good/bad reality. Children are too young to understand that objects can be both good and bad; they only see one part of the spectrum.

The formation of mental world is enabled by the infant-parent interpersonal interaction which was the main thesis of British object-relations tradition. Fairbairn also discovered the psychological condition of dysfunctional interpersonal attachment of abused children to their abusing parents. This area is linked to Attachment theory, which was developed by John Bowlby and which remains the primary theory of infant mental health. Children who are raised by abusive parents are at risk to abuse their children in some way when they grow up. Children who grow up in abusive families are at risk of having poor quality attachments to their parents.

Object Relations Psychotherapy is rooted in psychoanalytical principles. In addition there is not one type, but rather object relations theory is a guiding principle in various forms of object relations therapy. The most important difference between psychotherapy based on principles of object relations theory and psychoanalysis is that the therapist does not assume as passive a role as in traditional psychoanalysis, since the interpretation of the transference relationship, while important, is not such a central component. Instead, the therapist's role is to pay attention to ways in which the patient projects previous object relationships into the interactions with the therapist.

Most therapies incorporating object relations theory then conceptualise the therapy as helping the patient resolve the pathological qualities of the transference relationship through the active experience of the real relationship between the therapist and the patient. This re-experiencing of such vital object relational issues as intimacy, control, loss, transparency, dependency/ autonomy, and trust represents the primary curative influence. While some interpretation and confrontation may be involved, the "working through" of the original pathological components of the patient's emotional world and the objects in it is the primary therapeutic goal.

6.3.4. Structural Theory

The word ego was coined by Freud. The ego was composed of those forces that opposed the drives—defensive operations. The superego was Freud's term for the conscience—values and ideals, shame and guilt. Drives could be conscious or unconscious, and that consciousness vs. unconsciousness was a quality of any mental operation or any mental conflict. Forgetting things could be done on purpose, or not. People could be aware of guilt, or not aware.

6.3.5. Self Psychology

Self psychology explains psychopathology as being the result of disrupted or unmet developmental needs. Essential to understanding Self psychology are the concepts of empathy, self-object, mirroring, idealising, alter ego/twinship and the tripolar self. Though self psychology also recognises certain drives, conflicts and complexes present in Freudian psychodynamic theory, these are understood within a different framework.

6.3.6. Lacanian Psychoanalysis

Jaques Lacan, a French psychoanalyst is the brain behind this theory. It is a departure from the traditional British and American psychoanalysis. Lacan rejected attempts to link psychoanalysis with social theory, saying 'the unconscious is the discourse of the Other'—that human passion is structured by the desire of others and that we express deep feelings through the 'relay' of others. He thus saw desire as a social phenomenon and psychoanalysis as a theory of how the human subject is created through social interaction. Desire appears through a combination of language, culture and the spaces between people.

Lacan focused largely on Freud's work on deep structures and infant sexuality, and how the human subject becomes an 'other' through unconscious repression and stemming from the Mirror phase. The conscious ego and unconscious desire are thus radically divided. Lacan considered this perpetual and unconscious fragmentation of the self as Freud's core discovery.

Lacanian psychoanalysis is rather ruthless in its aggressive challenging that seeks to dismantle the imaginary sense of completeness and to remove illusions of self-mastery through a mirror image. A strong ego is seen as defensive deceit and expressing it during analysis is seen as resistance to change. Fear of disintegration and lack drives the person to realise themselves in another imaginary individual.

Language is used to represent desire and is an 'intersubjective order of symbolisation' and force that perpetuates the 'Law of the father.' The father prohibits the desire of the mother, subverting this desire into language.

6.3.7. Feminist Theory of Psychoanalysis

The main proponents of Feminist theory are Julia Kristeva, Luce Irigaray and Bracha Ettinger. Psychoanalytic feminism maintains that gender is not biological but is based on the psychosexual development of the individual. Psychoanalytical feminists believe that gender inequality comes from early childhood experiences, which lead men to believe themselves to be masculine, and women to believe themselves feminine. It is further maintained that gender leads to a social system that is dominated by males, which in turn influences the individual psychosexual development. As a solution it was suggested to avoid the gender-specific structuring of the society by male-female coeducation. In the last 30 years, the contemporary French psychoanalytical theories concerning the feminine, that refer to sexual difference rather than to gender, with psychoanalysts like Julia Kristeva, Luce Irigaray and Bracha L. Ettinger, has largely influenced not only feminist theory but also the understanding of the subject in philosophy and the general field of psychoanalysis itself.

6.3.8. Analytical Psychology

Carl Jung's analytical psychology is distinct from Freudian psychoanalysis but also has a number of similarities. Its aim is the apprehension and integration of the deep forces and motivations underlying human behaviour by the practice of an accumulative phenomenology around the significance of dreams, folklore and mythology. Depth psychology and archetypal psychology are related in that they both employ the model of the unconscious mind as the source of healing and development in the individual.

Jung developed his own distinctive approach to the study of the human mind. In his early years when working in a Swiss hospital with schizophrenic patients and working with Sigmund Freud and the burgeoning psychoanalytic community, he took a closer look at the mysterious depths of the human unconscious. Fascinated by what he saw he devoted his life to the exploration of the unconscious. Unlike many modern psychologists, Jung did not feel that experimenting using natural science was the best means to understand the soul. For him, an empirical investigation of the world of dream, myth, and soul represented the most promising road to deeper understanding.

The overarching goal of Jungian psychology is the reconciliation of the life of the individual with the world of the supra-personal archetypes. Central to this process is the individual's encounter with the unconscious. Humans experience the unconscious through symbols encountered in all aspects of life: in dreams, art, religion, and the symbolic dramas we enact in our relationships and life pursuits. Essential to the encounter with the unconscious, and the reconciliation of the individual's consciousness with this broader world, is learning this symbolic language. Only through attention and openness to this world is the individual able to harmonise their life with these suprapersonal archetypal forces.

In order to undergo the individuation process, the individual must be open to the parts of oneself beyond one's own ego. In order to do this, the modern individual must pay attention to dreams, explore the world of religion and spirituality, and question the assumptions of the operant societal worldview.

6.3.9. Interpersonal Psychoanalysis

Harry Stack Sullivan was the pioneer who introduced interpersonal psychoanalysis and it was further developed by Frieda Fromm-Reichmann. According to Sullivan patients keep many aspects of interpersonal relationships out of their awareness by selective inattention. He felt that it to be important for psychotherapists to conduct a detailed inquiry into patient's interactions with others so that patients would become optimally aware of their interpersonal patterns. Unlike classical psychoanalysts, interpersonal analysts focus on asking patients detailed questions about their moment-to-moment interactions with others, including the analyst.

6.3.10. Relational Psychoanalysis

Stephen Mitchell's relational psychoanalysis is a combination of interpersonal psychoanalysis with object-relations theory and with Inter-subjective theory as critical for mental health. It emphasises how the individual's personality is shaped by both real and imagined relationships with others, and how these relationship patterns are re-enacted in the interactions between analyst and patient. Fonagy and Target, in London, have propounded their view of the necessity of helping certain detached, isolated patients, develop the capacity for "mentalisation" associated with thinking about relationships and themselves.

This analysis originated in the 1980's as an attempt to integrate interpersonal psychoanalysis's emphasis on the detailed exploration of interpersonal interactions with British object relations theory's sophisticated ideas about the psychological importance of internalised relationships with other people. Relationalists argue that personality emerges out of the matrix of early formative relationships with parents and other figures. Philosophically, relational psychoanalysis is closely allied with social constructionism.

The main difference between relational theory and traditional psychoanalytic thought is its theory of motivation. Freudian theory, with a few exceptions, proposes that human beings are motivated by sexual and aggressive drives. These drives are biologically rooted and innate. They are ultimately not shaped by experience.

Relational psychoanalysts stress a mixture of waiting, and authentic spontaneity when treating patients. Some relationally oriented psychoanalysts eschew the traditional Freudian emphasis on interpretation and free association, instead emphasising the importance of creating a lively, genuine relationship with the patient.

Relational analysts feel that psychotherapy works best when the therapist focuses on establishing a healing relationship with the patient, in addition to focusing on facilitating insight. By doing so, therapists break patients out of the repetitive patterns of relating to others that they believe maintain psychopathology.

6.3.11. Modern Psychoanalysis

Modern psychoanalysis is a treatment for relieving mental and emotional distress. Its aim is to heal through the simple technique of verbal interaction between patient and therapist. Sigmund Freud used the psychoanalytic form of treatment for mental and emotional troubles in the early part of the 19th century. Later psychoanalysts expanded on Freud's work and enlarged the range of problems that could be treated. Modern Psychoanalysis is presented as utilising a wide range of interventions including ego reinforcement, emotional communication and resistance resolution. The theory of treatment in Modern Psychoanalysis considers most emotional, mental and personal achievement problems to be reversible through these techniques.

In psychoanalytic therapy, the analyst prefers to help the patient understand why he or she is unable to solve problems and internal conflicts that might be preventing one from knowing what to do in life.

The Modern Psychoanalytic treatment approach emphasises the development of the narcissistic transference in which the patient relates to the therapist as if he were part of his own mind, rather than a separate person. The theory is that most neuroses and severe mental illnesses originate in the premedical period, before the development of language. The transference that develops with these patients then is largely enacted nonverbally through behaviour, symptoms, symbolic communications and, importantly, the transmission of feeling states, otherwise known as induced feelings.

The narcissistic defence is considered central to most mental disturbances and is characterised by self-hate rather than self-love. Aggression is directed towards the self in order to protect the object. Treatment then emphasises helping patients to better metabolise their aggressive drives, by gradually being able to express their aggression in treatment.

6.3.12. Psychopathology

Psychopathology is developed to compensate the missing links in the earlier analyses. In depressions with psychotic features, the self-preservation function may also be damaged (sometimes by overwhelming depressive affect). Because of the integrative deficits, the development of self and object representations is also impaired. Clinically, therefore, psychotic individuals manifest limitations in warmth, empathy, trust, identity, closeness and/or stability in relationships (due to problems with self-object fusion anxiety) as well.

Psychopaths are the adults who do not experience guilt and shame, and who indulge in criminal behaviour. Panic, phobias, conversions, obsessions, compulsions and depressions (analysts call these "neurotic symptoms") are not usually caused by deficits in functions. Instead, they are caused by intrapsychic conflicts. The conflicts are generally among sexual and hostile-aggressive wishes, guilt and shame, and reality factors. The conflicts may be conscious or unconscious, but create anxiety, depressive affect, and anger.

The various elements are managed by defensive operations—essentially shut-off brain mechanisms that make people unaware of that element of conflict. "Repression" is the term given to the mechanism that shuts thoughts out of consciousness. "Isolation of affect" is the term used for the mechanism that shuts sensations out of consciousness. Neurotic symptoms may occur with or without deficits in ego functions, object relations, and ego strengths. Therefore, it is not uncommon to encounter obsessive-compulsive schizophrenics, panic patients who also suffer with borderline personality disorder, etc.

Many adult problems can trace their origins to unresolved conflicts from certain phases of childhood and adolescence. Freud, based on the data gathered from his patients early in his career, suspected that neurotic disturbances occurred when children were sexually abused in childhood. Although child abuse occurs, that not all neurotic symptoms were associated with this. Neurotic people often had unconscious conflicts that involved incestuous fantasies deriving from different stages of development.

Freud found the stage from about three to six years of age (preschool years, today called the "first genital stage") to be filled with fantasies about marriage with both parents. Although arguments were generated in early 20th-century Vienna about whether adult seduction of children was the basis of neurotic illness, there is virtually no argument about this problem in the 21st century.

The actual effects of child abuse include ego and object relations deficits and severe neurotic conflicts. Much research has been done on these types of trauma in childhood, and the adult sequelae of those. On the other hand, many adults with symptom neuroses and character pathology have no history of childhood sexual or physical abuse.

The term Oedipus complex or oedipal was first coined by Freud. It refers to the powerful attachments that children make to their parents in the preschool years. These attachments involve fantasies of marriage to either (or both) parent, and, therefore, competitive fantasies toward either (or both) parents. Humberto Nagera has been particularly helpful in clarifying many of the complexities of the child through these years.

There are "positive" and "negative" oedipal conflicts. These are attached to the heterosexual and homosexual aspects, respectively. Both seem to occur in development of most children. Eventually, the developing child's concessions to reality lead to identifications with parental values. These identifications generally create a new set of mental operations regarding values and guilt, subsumed under the term "superego." Besides superego development, children "resolve" their preschool oedipal conflicts through channelling wishes into something their parents approve of (sublimations) and the development, during the school-age years (latency) of age-appropriate obsessive-compulsive defensive maneuvers (rules, repetitive games).

6.4. Analytic Techniques in Treatment

Some of the mental illnesses are treated with analytical techniques. These are phobias, conversions, compulsions, obsessions, anxiety attacks, depressions, sexual dysfunctions, a wide variety of relationship problems (such as dating and marital strife), and a wide variety of character problems (painful shyness, meanness, obnoxiousness, workaholism, hyperseductiveness, hyperemotionality, hyperfastidiousness).

Psychoanalysis interprets unconscious conflicts that are interfering with current-day functioning—conflicts that are causing painful symptoms such as phobias, anxiety, depression, and compulsions. Strachey stressed that figuring out ways the patient distorted perceptions about the analyst led to understanding what may have been forgotten. In particular, unconscious hostile feelings toward the analyst could be found in symbolic, negative reactions to what Robert Langs later called the "frame" of the therapy—the setup that included times of the sessions, payment of fees, and necessity of talking. In patients who made mistakes, forgot, or showed other peculiarities regarding time, fees, and talking, the analyst can usually find various unconscious "resistances" to the flow of thoughts.

6.5. Conclusion

From the very beginning of human existence, people have tried to trace the ways mind travels. But still it is a mystery. It can travel anyway or anywhere. The sub conscious or unconscious mind is out of the control of a person. But the therapists who are trying to leash a mind with disorders put forward many theories. These theories help them to know the mind of others in a certain extend.

References

Burgin, Victor, James Donald and Cora Kaplan, eds., *Formations of Fantasy*, Routledge, 1989.

Juliet Mitchell and Jacqueline Rose (eds.), *Feminine Sexuality and the Ecole Freudienne*, Macmillan, 1982.

Lacan, Jacques, "Seminar XI: Four Fundamental Concepts of Psychoanalysis", *Trans. Alan Sheridan*, Penguin, 1986.

Laplanche, J. and J.-B. Pontalis, *The Language of Psychoanalysis*, London: Hogarth, 1973.

Stephen Frosh, "Social Repression," *The Politics of Psychoanalysis*, Macmillan, 1985.

7

Cognitive Therapy and Cognitive Behavioural Approaches

7.1. Cognitive Therapy

In 1960s, a psychiatrist called Aaron T. Beck propagated cognitive Therapy (CT) as a type of psychotherapy. Beck was very disappointed with long-term psychodynamic approaches based on gaining insight into unconscious emotions and drives. So, he came to the conclusion that the way in which his clients perceived and interpreted and attributed meaning-a process known scientifically as cognition-in their daily lives was a key to therapy. Albert Ellis was working on similar ideas from a different perspective, in developing his rational emotive behaviour therapy (REBT). Beck initially focused on depression and developed a list of "errors" in thinking that he proposed could cause or maintain depression, including arbitrary inference, selective abstraction, over-generalisation, and magnification (of negatives) and minimisation (of positives). Cognitive therapy seeks to identify and change "distorted" or "unrealistic" ways of thinking, and therefore to influence emotion and behaviour.

Beck also introduced a focus on the underlying "schema"-the fundamental underlying ways in which people process information-whether about the self, the world or the future. Treatment is based on collaboration between client and therapist and on testing beliefs.

Behaviourism was the fast gripping theory during those days. But the new cognitive approach came into conflict with this behaviourism, which denied that talk of mental causes was scientific or meaningful, rather than simply assessing stimuli and behavioural responses. However, the 1970s saw a general "cognitive revolution" in psychology. Behavioural modification techniques and cognitive therapy techniques became joined together, giving rise to cognitive behavioural therapy. The term is sometimes used interchangeably with cognitive therapy, since cognitive therapy has always included some behavioural components, but advocates of Beck's particular approach seek to maintain and establish its integrity as a distinct clearly-standardised kind of cognitive behavioural therapy.

The central insight of cognitive therapy as originally formulated over three decades ago is that thoughts mediate between stimuli, such as external events, and emotions. A stimulus elicits a thought—which might be an evaluative judgement of some kind—which in turn gives rise to an emotion. In other words, it is not the stimulus itself which somehow elicits an emotional response directly, but our evaluation of or thought about that stimulus. Two ancillary assumptions underpin the approach of the cognitive therapist:

1) The client is capable of becoming aware of his or her own thoughts and of changing them, and
2) Sometimes the thoughts elicited by stimuli distort or otherwise fail to reflect reality accurately.

As per cognitive therapy, psychological distress is caused by distorted thoughts about stimuli giving rise to distressed emotions. The theory is particularly well developed in the case of depression, where clients frequently experience unduly negative thoughts which arise automatically even in response to stimuli which might otherwise be experienced as positive. Usually cognitive therapeutic work is informed by an awareness of the role of the client's behaviour as well.

The task of cognitive therapy or CBT is partly to understand how the three components of emotions, behaviours and thoughts interrelate, and how they may be influenced by external stimuli—including events which may have occurred early in the client's life.

7.1.1. Therapeutic Approach of Cognitive Therapy

Thought distortions are the major cause of psychological distresses. The cognitive therapy aims to help the client to become aware of such thought distortions. But it doesn't mean that every distortion can be corrected by cognitive therapy. After all, virtually everyone distorts reality in many ways—just those which may be at the root of distress. The therapist will make every effort to understand experiences from the client's point of view, and the client and therapist will work collaboratively with an empirical spirit, like scientists, exploring the client's thoughts, assumptions and inferences. The therapist helps the client learn to test these by checking them against reality and against other assumptions. Often this process will continue outside the therapeutic session.

Therapeutic interventions frequently involve the client's behaviour because of the interrelationship between thoughts, feelings and behaviours. For instance, a client with a strong fear that squirrels will jump onto their head if they walk under trees may go to great lengths to avoid walking under trees. This behaviour will prevent the client from acquiring information that contradicts their thought that "if I walk under a tree, a squirrel will jump onto my head" or perhaps their mental image of a squirrel jumping onto their head the moment they step under a tree. The therapist may help the client to overcome this avoidance of walking under trees as part of the process of correcting the distorted thought that walking under trees will lead to squirrels jumping on the client's head.

Throughout this process of learning, exploring and testing, the client acquires coping strategies as well as improved skills of awareness, introspection and evaluation. This enables them to manage the process on their own in the future, reducing their reliance on the therapist and reducing the likelihood of experiencing a relapse.

7.2. Cognitive Behavioural Therapy (CBT)

A cognitive behavioural therapy is a psychotherapy based on modifying cognitions, assumptions, beliefs and behaviours, with the aim of influencing disturbed emotions. The general approach, developed out of behaviour modification, cognitive therapy and rational emotive behaviour therapy, has become widely used to treat various kinds of neuroses and psychopathology, including mood disorders and anxiety disorders.

According to the nature of client, the particular therapeutic techniques may vary, but commonly include keeping a diary of significant events and associated feelings, thoughts and behaviours; questioning and testing cognitions, assumptions, evaluations and beliefs that might be unhelpful and unrealistic; gradually facing activities which may have been avoided; and trying out new ways of behaving and reacting. Relaxation and distraction techniques are also commonly included.

CBT is widely accepted as an evidence- and empiricism-based, cost-effective psychotherapy for many disorders and psychological problems. It is sometimes used with groups of people as well as individuals, and the techniques are also commonly adapted for self-help manuals and, increasingly, for self-help software packages.

The most common behaviour of a depressed person is that, he may think he is useless. This, in turn, worsens the mood, leading to feelings of depression; the problem may be worsened if the individual reacts by avoiding activities and then behaviourally confirming his negative belief to himself. As a result, a successful experience becomes more unlikely, which reinforces the original thought of being "useless."

In therapy, the latter example could be identified as a self-fulfilling prophecy or "problem cycle," and the efforts of the therapist and client would be directed at working together to change this. This is done by addressing the way the client thinks and behaves in response to similar situations and by developing more flexible ways to think and respond, including reducing the avoidance of activities. If, as a result, the client escapes the negative thought patterns and destructive behaviours, the feelings of depression may, over time, be relieved. The client may then become more active, succeed more often, and further reduce feelings of depression.

The objectives of CBT typically are to identify irrational or maladaptive thoughts, assumptions and beliefs that are related to debilitating negative emotions and to identify how they are dysfunctional, inaccurate, or simply not helpful. This is done in an effort to reject the distorted cognitions and to replace them with more realistic and self-helping alternatives.

Cognitive behavioural therapy is not an overnight process. Even after patients have learned to recognise when and where their mental processes go awry, it can take months of effort to replace any dysfunctional cognitive-affective-behavioural processes or habit with a more reasonable, salutary one.

A person's core beliefs (often formed in childhood) contribute to "automatic thoughts" that pop up in everyday life in response to situations. Cognitive therapy practitioners hold that clinical depression is typically associated with negatively biased thinking and irrational thoughts. This therapy is often used in conjunction with mood stabilising medications to treat bipolar disorder.

Cognitive Behavioural Group Therapy (CBGT) is a similar approach in treating mental illnesses, based on the protocol by Richard Heimberg. In this case, clients participate in a group and recognise they are not alone in suffering from their problems.

A sub-field of cognitive behavioural therapy used to treat Obsessive Compulsive Disorder makes use of classical conditioning through extinction (a type of conditioning) and habituation. CBT has also been successfully applied to the treatment of Generalised Anxiety Disorder, health anxiety, Social phobia and Panic Disorder.

Other types of Cognitive Behavioural Therapy include Dialectical Behaviour Therapy, Self-Instructional Training, Schema-Focused Therapy and many others. The cognitive behavioural therapy is very effective in reducing symptoms and preventing relapse.

7.3. Depression

When a person always thinks negatively, he is in depression. The depressed person can experience negative thoughts as being beyond their control, thereby allowing them to become automatic and self-perpetuating. Pessimistic thinking can be categorised into a number of common patterns called "cognitive distortions." The cognitive therapist provides techniques to give the client a greater degree of control over negative thinking by correcting these distortions or correcting thinking errors that abet the distortions, in a process called cognitive restructuring.

There are a lot of factors leads a person into the state of depression. Aaron Beck's cognitive theory of depression is regarded as the most verified psychological theory of depression. His theory states that depressed people think the way they do because their thinking is biased towards negative interpretations. According to Beck's theory of the etiology of depression, depressed people acquire a negative schema of the world in childhood and adolescence. Depressed people acquire such schemas through a loss of a parent, rejection of peers, criticism from teachers or parents, the depressive attitude of a parent and other negative events. When the person with such schemas encounters a situation that resembles in some way, even remotely, the conditions in which the original schema was learned, the negative schemas of the person are activated.

Beck also included a negative triad in his theory. A negative triad is made up of the negative schemas and cognitive biases of the person. A cognitive bias is a view of the world. Depressed people, according to this theory, have views such as "I never do a good job."

A negative schema helps give rise to the cognitive bias, and the cognitive bias helps fuel the negative schema. This is the negative triad. Depressed people often have the following cognitive biases: arbitrary inference, selective abstraction, overgeneralisation, magnification and minimisation. These cognitive biases are quick to make negative, generalised, and personal inferences of the self, thus fueling the negative schema.

Hopelessness theory of depression is another cognitive theory of depression. This is the latest theory of the helpless/hopeless theories of depression. According to this theory, hopelessness depression is caused by a state of hopelessness. A state of hopelessness obtains when the person believes that no good outcomes will happen and that bad ones will happen instead. Also, the person feels that he or she has no ability to change the situation so that good things will happen. Stressors (negative life events) are thought to interact with a diathesis to create a sense of hopelessness.

Some proposed diatheses are attributing negative events to stable and global factors, low self-esteem, and a tendency to believe that negative life events will have severe negative consequences. Such diatheses increase the possibility that a person will experience hopelessness depression.

7.3.1. Attributional Style

In 1978, Lyn Abramson proposed the attributional style in depression. Depression based on attribution theory in social psychology is related to the concept of attributional style. This approach argues that depressives have a typical attributional style -they tend to attribute negative events in their lives to stable and global characteristics of themselves. This theory is sometimes known as a revised version of learned helplessness theory.

Later, in 1989, this theory was challenged by Hopelessness Theory. This theory emphasised attributions to global and stable factors, rather than, as in the original model, internal attributions. Hopelessness Theory also emphasises that beliefs about the consequences of events, and rated importance of events, may be at least as important as causal attributions in understanding why some people react to negative events with clinical depression.

7.3.2. ABCs of Irrational Beliefs

ABC Technique of Irrational Beliefs is a major aid in cognitive therapy. The first three steps analyse the process by which a person has developed irrational beliefs. They are:

A—Activating Event or objective situation: The objective situation is an event that ultimately leads to some type of high emotional response or negative dysfunctional thinking.

B—Beliefs: Here, the client writes down the negative thoughts that occurred to him or her.

C—Consequence: This is for the negative disturbed feelings and dysfunctional behaviours that ensued. The negative thoughts of the second column are seen as a connecting bridge between the situation and the distressing feelings.

After irrational beliefs have been identified, the therapist will often work with the client in challenging the negative thoughts on the basis of evidence from the client's experience by reframing it, meaning to i it in a more realistic light. This helps the client to develop more rational beliefs and healthy coping strategies.

7.3.3. CBT with children and Youths

Cognitive behavioural therapy is a good medicine for treating depression in children and youths. It is often used to treat depression, anxiety disorders, and symptoms related to trauma and Post Traumatic Stress Disorder.

7.3.4. Computerised CBT

This is a computerised form of CBT, in which the user interacts with computer software, instead of face to face with a therapist. Computerised CBT is not a replacement for face-to-face therapy but can provide an option for patients, especially in light of the fact that there are not always therapists available, or the cost can be prohibitive.

7.4. Criticisms of Cognitive Therapy and CBT

The main criticism against the cognitive therapeutic approach is that, many people will observe that simply being told that a view doesn't accurately reflect reality doesn't actually make them feel any better. A cognitive therapist merely tells the client something is wrong is to caricature the approach.

7.5. Conclusion

Depression, anxiety, panic and obsessive-compulsive disorder, etc are a state of mind. To find a way out from this disorders need effective medication. Cognitive and cognitive behavioural theories approach a diseased mind with a loving touch. The thoughts of aloneness and helplessness will directly land a person into depression. Through these approaches, the therapist tries to enter into the mind of depressed person and take out the negative thoughts. A personal touch is essential for everybody to lead this stressful life.

References

Henin, A., Warman, M., & Kendall, P. C., "Cognitive-behavioral therapy with children and adolescents", In G. Simos (Ed.) *Cognitive behavior therapy: A guide for the practicing clinician*, East Sussex: Brunner-Routledge, 2002.

Kendall, P. C., Choudhury, M., Chung, H., & Robin, J., "Cognitive-behavioral approaches", In M. Lewis (Ed.) *Child and adolescent psychiatry* (3(rd) ed.), Baltimore, MD: Lippincott Williams & Wilkins. 2002.

8

Existential Counselling and Psychotherapy

8.1. Introduction

Existential approaches to counselling and psychotherapy focus on exploring the challenges and paradoxes of human existence, rather than psychopathology. Personality derives from thoughts and attitude. The existential approach characterises human beings as creatures of continual change and transformation, living essentially finite lives in a context of personal strengths and weaknesses as well as opportunities and limitations created by their environment. With attention given to this entire context of the client's life, the existential approach is all about exploring meaning and value and learning to live authentically—that is, in accordance with one's own ideals, priorities and values. Authentic living means being true to oneself and honest about one's own possibilities and limitations, continually creating one's own identity even in the face of deep uncertainty about everything in the future except for the eventual arrival of our own death. In other words, authentic living is living deliberately, rather than by default.

Life is very complex. But the success of life depends on a person's ability to overcome complexities. Psychological health, from an existential perspective, is characterised by an ability to navigate the complexities of one's own life, the world, and one's relationships with the world. Disturbance, on the other hand, is taken as the outcome of avoiding life's truths and of working under the shadow of other people's expectations and values. Self deception about these factors provides a powerful psychological defence mechanism. Existential counselling maintains that disturbance is an inevitable experience for virtually everyone; the question is not so much how to avoid it as it is how to face it with openness and a willingness to engage with life rather than a tendency to retreat, withdraw or refrain from responsibility.

8.2. Existential Therapy

The deep thoughts may end a person in a conclusion that he is alone in this vast world. Existential psychotherapy is partly based on this belief of a person. This aloneness leads to feelings of meaninglessness which can be overcome only by creating one's own values and meanings.

We have the power to create because we have the freedom to choose. In making our own choices we assume full responsibility for the results and blame no one but ourselves if the result is less than what was desired. The psychotherapist helps his or her patients/clients along this path: to discover why the patient/client is overburdened by the anxieties of aloneness and meaninglessness, to find new and better ways to manage these anxieties, to make new and healthy choices, and to emerge from therapy as a free and sound human being.

8.2.1. Evolution of the Existential Theory

When a person ponders over and over about his aloneness, it will damage his positive thinking capacity. Existential therapy focuses on the development of a patient/client's self-awareness by looking deeply into the issues of our aloneness, meaninglessness, and mortality. The therapist emphasises the historical background to this approach is that of 3,000 years of philosophy.

Since the existence of mankind, people have tried to make sense of life in general and of their personal predicaments in particular. Much of the philosophical tradition is relevant and can help us to understand an individual's position in the world. The philosophers who are especially pertinent are those whose work is directly aimed at making sense of human existence. But the philosophical movements that are of most importance and that have been directly responsible for the generation of existential therapy are phenomenology and existential philosophy.

However, the existential philosophy showed its strong presence in the last century and the work of Kierkegaard and Nietzsche. Both were in conflict with the predominant ideologies of their time and committed to the exploration of reality as it can be experienced in a passionate and personal manner.

The theory of Kierkegaard was a vigorous protest against Christian dogma and the so-called 'objectivity' of science. He thought that both were ways of avoiding the anxiety inherent in human existence. He had great contempt for the way in which life was being lived by those around him and believed that truth could ultimately only be discovered subjectively by the individual in action.

Kierkegaard was of the opinion that people lacks courage to take the leap of faith and live with passion and commitment from the inward depth of existence. This involved a constant struggle between the finite and infinite aspects of our nature as part of the difficult task of creating a self and finding meaning. As Kierkegaard lived by his own word he was lonely and much ridiculed during his lifetime.

Nietzsche gave a further mileage to Kierkegaard's philosophy and told that God was dead and that it is up to us to re-evaluate existence in light of this. He invited people to shake off the shackles of moral constraint and to discover their free will in order to soar to unknown heights and learn to live with new intensity. He encouraged people not to remain part of the herd, but to dare stand out. The important existential themes of freedom, choice, responsibility and courage are introduced for the first time.

Kierkegaard and Nietzsche stick on the human issues that needed to be addressed. But Husserl's phenomenology provided the method to address them in a rigorous manner. He contended that natural sciences are based on the assumption that subject and object are separate and that this kind of dualism can only lead to error. He proposed a whole new mode of investigation and understanding of the world and our experience of it. Prejudice has to be put aside or 'bracketed,' in order for us to meet the world afresh and discover what is absolutely fundamental and only directly available to us through intuition. If we want to grasp the essence of things, instead of explaining and analysing them we have to learn to describe and understand them.

Phenomenological method to understanding the meaning of being was the philosophy of Heidegger. According to him, "Poetry and deep philosophical thinking can bring greater insight into what it means to be in the world than can be achieved through scientific knowledge. Human being in the world in a manner revolutionises classical ideas about the self and psychology." He recognised the importance of time, space, death and human relatedness. He also favoured hermeneutics, an old philosophical method of investigation, which is the art of interpretation. Unlike interpretation as practised in psychoanalysis this kind of interpretation seeks to understand how the person himself subjectively experiences something.

Sartre contributed many other strands of existential exploration, particularly in terms of emotions, imagination, and the person's insertion into a social and political world. He became the father of existentialism, which was a philosophical trend with a limited life span. The philosophy of existence on the contrary is carried by a wide-ranging literature, which includes many other authors than the ones mentioned above. Psychotherapy has traditionally grown within a medical rather than a philosophical milieu and is only just beginning to discover the possibility of a radical philosophical approach.

However, phenomenology and its possibilities for working with people inspired some psychotherapists in the beginning of the 20th century. Ludwig Binswanger, in Switzerland, was the first to attempt to bring existential insights to his work with patients, in the Kreuzlingen sanatorium where he was a psychiatrist. This had a considerable impact on the popularisation of existential ideas as a basis for therapy. Rollo May played an important role in this, and his writing kept the existential influence alive in America, leading eventually to a specific formulation of therapy. Humanistic psychology was directly influenced by these ideas, but it invariably diluted and sometimes distorted their original meanings.

By associating with Heidegger, European psychologist Medard Boss developed existential ideas were combined with some psychoanalytic principles and a method of existential analysis. In Austria, Viktor Frankl developed an existential therapy called logotherapy, which focused particularly on finding meaning. In France the ideas of Sartre and Merleau-Ponty and of a number of practitioners were important and influential but no specific therapeutic method was developed from them.

Existential approach flourished in Britain when R.D. Laing and David Cooper, often associated with the anti-psychiatry movement, took Sartre's existential ideas as the basis for their work. Without developing a concrete method of therapy they critically reconsidered the notion of mental illness and its treatment. In the late 1960s they established an experimental therapeutic community at Kingsley Hall in the East End of London, where people could come to live through their madness without the usual medical treatment. They also founded the Philadelphia Association, an organisation providing alternative living, therapy and therapeutic training from this perspective.

The cropping up of existentially based courses in academic institutions gave further impetus for the development of the existential approach in Britain. In the last decades the existential approach has spread rapidly and has become a welcome alternative to established methods. There are now a number of other, mostly academic, centres in Britain that provide training in existential counselling and psychotherapy and a rapidly growing interest in the approach in the voluntary sector and in the National Health Service.

8.2.2. Understanding Human Mind

It is true that all human beings are alone in this world. But the life of everybody is connected to others. We want to have meaning in their lives while they have meaning in ours, but ultimately we must come to realise that we cannot depend on others for our validation, and with that realisation we finally acknowledge and understand that we are fundamentally alone. The result of this revelation is anxiety in the knowledge that our validation must come from within and not from others.

Human beings are social animals. The life of all people is interrelated. Leading an alienated and isolated life is meaningless. Nothing exists which is greater than ourselves, therefore there are no external sources of values and absolutes from which we can draw. Taken to an extreme, we might conclude that there is nothing for which to live. However, we also possess the freedom to create our own values and personal life-meaning, and apply them to our condition. This freedom gives us feelings of significance and purpose that are strong enough to carry us through life. Still, the freedom to choose is another source of anxiety: we must summon the requisite strength and courage to choose our personal life-meaning and hold fast to it. This is undoubtedly a task which many find difficult.

If there is a life, there is death also. Nobody can stay in this world for ever. One day, all have to leave this world. This feeling may create anxiety and fears in the mind of people. At some point in the future we will cease to be, while frightening, is at the same time invigorating because it is relevant right now. The juxtaposition of life and death is one thing that does give us some certainty.

Humans are responsible. Being isolated, alone, and free to choose means that one cannot assign blame for his or her problems to someone else. The individual alone makes the choices and therefore is responsible for the outcomes. At any point we are free to make different choices and thus re-invent ourselves; we are at once the architect, the planner, and the builder of our lives, throughout our lives.

8.2.3. Psychological Dysfunction

We all have the freedom to lead our life in our own way. However one may feel unable to come to terms with the anxiety of being alone in the world. If so an existential psychotherapist can assist one in accepting these feelings rather than trying to change them as if there is something wrong. Everyone has the freedom to choose how they are going to be in life, however this may go unexercised because making changes is difficult; it may appear easier and safer not to make decisions that you will be responsible for. Many people will remain unaware of alternative choices in life for various societal reasons.

8.2.4. Ways to a Peaceful Life

The peace or misery in life of a person is determined by his mental prowess. Life is always stressful. It is very hard to get a tension free life. But if a person is courageous enough to face the anxieties of life, mental peace will be with such people. They courageously take the helm of their lives and steer in whatever direction they choose; they have the courage to be. One does not need to arrest feelings of meaninglessness, but can choose new meanings for their lives. By building, by loving, and by creating one is able to live life as one's own adventure. One can accept one's own mortality and overcome fear of death.

8.2.5. Treating Mental Illness Using Existential Therapy

The psychotherapists, who follow existentially-oriented therapy for treating mental illness, triy to wipe off anxieties in the minds of their clients. If the client has not been fully exercising the freedom to choose, the counsellor will lead a discovering into how and why he or she is stuck. The client may have been allowing others to make important decisions which he or she alone should be making, or the client may be afraid to take the risks required to grow and is instead choosing an easy and non-threatening path.

Human mind has immense power. Mind itself is a healer also. For this, a person should change his way of thinking. If the thinking is proper, people will find a way by their own to cope with the aloneness and meaninglessness of life. The counsellor does not try to eliminate these anxieties, but instead encourages the client to face them head-on. Alternative paths can be explored together. The risks entailed with these paths can be evaluated, and the client will then be able to make new, more authentic choices.

Past is past. The existential psychotherapist also gives emphasis on the present and future. The counsellor and the client may reflect upon how the client has answered life's questions in the past, but attention ultimately shifts to searching for a new and increased awareness in the present and enabling a new freedom and responsibility to act. The patient can then accept they are not special, and that their existence is simply coincidental, without destiny or fate. By accepting this, they can overcome their anxieties, and instead view life as moments, in which they are fundamentally free.

8.2.6. Basic Dimensions of Human Existence

Restrictive models categorise or label people, so it should be avoided. So, psychotherapists look for the universals that can be observed cross-culturally. There is no existential personality theory which divides humanity into types or reduces people to part components. Instead there is a description of the different levels of experience and existence with which people are inevitably confronted. The way in which a person is in the world at a particular stage can be charted on this general map of human existence. One can distinguish four basic dimensions of human existence: the physical, the social, the psychological and the spiritual.

Each of these dimensions, people encounter the world and shape their attitude out of their particular take on their experience. Our orientation towards the world defines our reality. The four dimensions are obviously interwoven and provide a complex four dimensional force field for our existence.

8.2.6.1. Physical Dimension

In this dimension, the focus is on our environment and to the givens of the natural world around us. This includes our attitude to the body we have, to the concrete surroundings we find ourselves in, to the climate and the weather, to objects and material possessions, to the bodies of other people, our own bodily needs, to health and illness and to our own mortality.

The struggle on this dimension is, in general terms, between the search for domination over the elements and natural law (as in technology, or in sports) and the need to accept the limitations of natural boundaries (as in ecology or old age). While people generally aim for security on this dimension (through health and wealth), it brings disillusionment and realisation because such security can only be temporary. Recognising limitations can bring great release of tension.

8.2.6.2. Social Dimension

Comparison with others and interaction with the public around us comes under social dimension. This dimension includes our response to the culture we live in, as well as to the class and race we belong to. Attitudes here range from love to hate and from co-operation to competition. The dynamic contradictions can be understood in terms of acceptance versus rejection or belonging versus isolation.

Some people prefer to withdraw from the world of others as much as possible. Others blindly chase public acceptance by going along with the rules and fashions of the moment. Otherwise they try to rise above these by becoming trendsetters themselves. By acquiring fame or other forms of power, we can attain dominance over others temporarily. Sooner or later we are, however, all confronted with both failure and aloneness.

8.2.6.3. Psychological Dimension

People create a world for their own in the psychological dimension. Views about our character, our past experience and our future possibilities are also important here. Here, people are aware about their strengths and weaknesses. They search for a sense of identity, a feeling of being substantial and having a self. But inevitably many events will confront us with evidence to the contrary and plunge us into a state of confusion or disintegration. Activity and passivity are an important polarity here.

Self-affirmation and resolution go with the former and surrender and yielding with the latter. Facing the final dissolution of self that comes with personal loss and the facing of death might bring anxiety and confusion to many who have not yet given up their sense of self-importance.

8.2.6.4. Spiritual Dimension

This is the world of spirituality. Here, we create a sense of an ideal world, an ideology and a philosophical outlook. It is here that we find meaning by putting all the pieces of the puzzle together for ourselves. For some people this is done by adhering to a religion or other prescriptive world view, for others it is about discovering or attributing meaning in a more secular or personal way. The contradictions that have to be faced on this dimension are often related to the tension between purpose and absurdity, hope and despair.

People create their values in search of something that matters enough to live or die for, something that may even have ultimate and universal validity. Usually the aim is the conquest of a soul, or something that will substantially surpass mortality. Facing the void and the possibility of nothingness are the indispensable counterparts of this quest for the eternal.

8.2.7. Therapeutic Approach

Inculcating values of life in clients is the major role of the existential therapists. The therapist is concerned to engage seriously with what matters most to the client, to avoid imposing their own judgements, and to help the client to elucidate and elaborate on their own perspective, with an ultimate view to the client's being able to live life well and in their own way.

The therapists are also human beings and so their thoughts are also may be biased and prejudiced. The therapist must be self aware and able to set aside as much as possible their pre-conceptions and to encounter the client's world with an open mind. The therapist brings a sort of deliberate naivete to the therapeutic relationship, with a goal of understanding the client's meaning rather than their own and recognising the client's assumptions and underlying life themes with a clarity which the client may not yet be able to muster.

The therapist will be sensitive to and help the client explore their weaknesses, limitations and responsibilities as well as their strengths, opportunities and freedoms. Above all, they will value the meaning which the client creates in their own emotions, thoughts, beliefs, and personal history. While exploring the client's world, the therapist may appeal to a 4-part framework encompassing the client's existence in the physical dimension of the natural world, the body, health and illness; the social dimension of public relationships; the psychological or personal dimension, where we experience our relationship with ourselves as well as intimacy with others; and the spiritual dimension of ideals, philosophy and ultimate meaning. This framework of four dimensions is not imposed on the client by the therapist; it simply informs the therapist's understanding of the client's world so that, for instance, if a client never mentioned intimate relationships, the therapist would become aware of a deficiency in their understanding of the client's personal dimension.

The existential approach seeks clarity and meaning in all these dimensions and thus, in a sense, it begins with a significantly broader view of human existence than those approaches which focus on specific psychological mechanisms or which focus on the self as a meaningful entity, separable from its relations and interactions with the surrounding world.

8.3. Evaluation of Existential Counselling

Existential Counselling give priority to 'intellectualising' the client's life situation. This characterisation is on target only to the extent that reflection, self examination, and self awareness are 'intellectual' activities. Some argues that the approach is not about intellectualising, but about verbalising the basic impressions, ideas, intuitions and feelings a person has about life.

The quality of existential counselling means that it is perhaps more narrow than some other approaches in terms of the client set whose concerns it can most successfully address. This criticism cuts both ways, and many other approaches may be less able to help clients who specifically approach life with something like the spirit favoured by existential counselling.

Whatever may be the criticism, clients who view their problems as challenges of living, rather than symptoms of psychopathology, and clients who are genuinely attracted to increasing self awareness and self examination, will be well served by existential counselling. The approach will appeal to clients who are interested in the search for meaning and in deeply personal philosophical investigations. The approach is well suited to those who are attempting to clarify their own personal ideology and/or those who are facing significant personal adversity or change; some existential practitioners suggest the approach is particularly appropriate for those who feel at the very edge of existence, including those with terminal illnesses or who are contemplating suicide, or perhaps those who are just beginning a new phase of life in some way.

8.4. Conclusion

Mental disturbances is a common problem every individual process. When the things are not favourable, the life of human beings ends up in misery. So, keeping a hilarious and healthy mind is inevitable for attaining mental peace. Everybody craves for such a mental state. But the peace goes with those who have the capacity to face the difficulties in life. Existential counselling and psychotherapy teach a person how to cope up with tensions in life.

References

Binswanger, L., "The Existential Analysis school of thought", in *Existence,* ed. May, R., Angel, E., Ellenberger, H.F., New York, Basic Books, 1958.

Boss, M., "Anxiety, Guilt and Psychotherapeutic Liberation" *Review of Existential Psychology and Psychiatry*, Vol 11, no.3, Sept. 1962.

________________., *Existential Foundations of Medicine and Psychology*, New York, Jason Aronson, 1979.

Cohn, H., *Existential Thought and Therapeutic Practice*, London: Sage, 1997.

Deurzen E. van., *Existential Counselling in Practice*, London: Sage Publications, 2nd edition 2002.

9
Psychodynamics

9.1. Introduction

Psychodynamics is the psychology of mental or emotional forces or processes developing especially in early childhood and their effects on behaviour and mental states. In other words, it is the study of human behaviour from the point of view of motivation and drives, depending largely on the functional significance of emotion, and based on the assumption that an individual's total personality and reactions at any given time are the product of the interaction between their conscious/unconscious mind, genetic constitution and their environment.

The explanation given by medical field on psychodynamics is the systematised study and theory of the psychological forces that underlie human behaviour, emphasising the interplay between unconscious and conscious motivation and the functional significance of emotion. This concept originally developed by Sigmund Freud. According to him, "Psychological processes are flows of psychological energy in a complex brain, establishing "psychodynamics" on the basis of psychological energy, ie, libido."

Psychodynamics or the dynamic psychology, studies the interrelationship of various parts of the mind, personality, or psyche as they relate to mental, emotional, or motivational forces especially at the unconscious level. There are two mental forces in psychodynamics. They are:

a) Interaction of emotional forces: the interaction of the emotional and motivational forces that affect behaviour and mental states, especially on a subconscious level;

b) Inner forces affecting behaviour: the study of the emotional and motivational forces that affect behaviour and states of mind.

As per Freud, psychological energy was constant (hence, emotional changes consisted only in displacements) and that it tended to rest (point attractor) through discharge (catharsis).

The mate selection psychology defines psychodynamics as the study of the forces, motives, and energy generated by the deepest of human needs. Generally, it is the study of transformations and exchanges of "psychic energy" within the personality. A focus in psychodynamics is the connection between the energetic of emotional states in the id, ego, and superego as they relate to early childhood developments and processes.

9.1.1. Freudian Concept of Psychodynamics

In Freudian concept, at the heart of psychological processes is the ego, which he envisions as battling with three forces: the id, the super-ego, and the outside world. Hence, the basic psychodynamic model focuses on the dynamic interactions between the id, ego, and superego. Psychodynamics, subsequently, attempts to explain or interpret behaviour or mental states in terms of innate emotional forces or processes.

Freud's greatest achievement in the field of psychodynamics was his concept that a dynamic psychology is one that studies the transformations and exchanges of energy within the personality. Freud's basic psychodynamic model focuses on the dynamic interactions between the id, ego, and superego. Psychodynamics, subsequently, attempts to explain or interpret behaviour or mental states in terms of innate emotional forces or processes.

Freud's daughter Anna Freud began to apply Freud's psychodynamic theories of the "ego" in 1930s, to the study of parent-child attachment and especially deprivation and in doing so developed ego psychology.

9.1.2. Jungian Concept of Psychodynamics

Carl Jung, the 20th century psychologists was of the view that there is a core tendency toward wholeness and balance within oneself and these core characteristics of the self are the ego, the personal unconscious, the collective unconscious, and archetypes.

9.1.3. Positive Psychology

In positive psychology, the psychodynamic conception of flow is defined as a conscious state of mind in harmonious order. In simple terms, it is a state in which people are so involved in an activity that nothing else seems to matter; the experience itself is so enjoyable that people will do it even at great costs, for the sake of doing it. In other words, in positive psychology, flow is a state of mental activity or operation in which the person is fully immersed in what he or she is doing, characterised by energised focus, full involvement, and success in the process of the activity.

9.2. Fundamentals in Psychodynamic Concepts

9.2.1. Unconscious

Unconscious is a mental experience in which a person loses control of normal awareness. The term is used to refer both to process (mental activity) and to an area of mental experience. There may be different levels of unconscious mental activity; from "unwilling to acknowledge" to "totally unaware."

Mind distinguishes unconscious activity from reflexes and learned behaviours. Unconscious thought processes may obey different rules of logic.

The term prescriptively unconscious or preconscious stands for memories, information and learned skills which are readily accessible, if not normally present in the mind. These aspects are subject to the same rules as conscious thoughts, and may be suppressed. On the other hand, dynamically unconscious refers to memories, fantasies, thoughts, feelings, wishes or impulses which may be actively repressed because they are unthinkable (conflicts with our view of ourselves and what is acceptable; causes too much anxiety, guilt or psychic pain).

The topographical model of Freud is a description of the parts of the mind that function at different levels of consciousness awareness. It refers to the quality of mental processes rather than their function. The structural model refers to three component parts of the personality; the id, ego and superego. These have motivational, interactive and executive functions consequent on mental processes.

When considering intrapsychic processes, the psychoanalytic model works well, but is not as much concerned with wider interpersonal phenomena. A person is always within a family within society. These systems interact with each other, and disturbance can be found at any or all levels. A wider social formulation allows conceptualisation of organisation of all levels.

9.2.2. Conflict

Conflicts can occur in many ways. It may be a conflict between one's own opposing feelings, between one's own inner and outer worlds, or from the external world being internalised and experienced as self or between the experience of different parts of one's own self.

Conflicts occur in interpersonal relations also. People seek help with symptoms or problems when they're in conflict over unacceptable aspects of themselves or their relationships. Can be conflict between impulses (e.g. libidinal vs. aggressive) or structures (e.g. ego vs. id).

The central dynamic concept of conflict related to primitive impulses, urges and fantasies (the forces behind these are experienced as coming from deep within). Conflict is the failure to come to terms with these vital parts of our nature. Opposition, often unconscious, between opposing wishes or fears (e.g. wish to be angry but fear of being punished in response). Thus different parts of the mind are active and affect behaviour.

The conflicts become neurotic only when one aspect is unconscious and it is resolved by other than mature defences. Conflicts may be active at any level from the fully conscious to the totally unconscious.

9.2.3. Motivation

The psychoanalytic theory drives are the fundamental reasons behind human motivation—love, hate, heroism, destructiveness. All psychological theories need to explain motivation. Psychotherapists are not much concerned with innate behaviour (simple reflexes to complex patterns) or basic needs (food, water, air). Although these powerfully motivate behaviour if unsatisfied they are not the province of psychotherapy. Psychoanalytic psychotherapists are more concerned about motivational forces that cause conflict.

9.2.4. Drives

Basic drives are associated with human behaviours such as sexual, aggressive, feeding, attachment, parental, social, curiosity/ exploration, etc. Drives may lead to unacceptable wishes, feelings, and memories. These can be unacceptable because of conflict between socialisation (what we have been taught is right) and gratification (the internal need to fulfill a drive). This can lead to feelings of alienation from some part of oneself.

9.2.5. Ingredients of Mind

Human mind is guided by thoughts and emotions. If such feelings appear beyond certain limit, it becomes a disorder.

9.2.5.1. Ego

Ego is the organised part of psyche and it is the home of reason and common sense—rational thinking, external perception, and voluntary activity. It is also the site of defence mechanisms, which are felt to protect the ego.

Ego is is an original integrated part of the psyche and it refers to objective structure, not to an objective experiential phenomenon (self). It is the centre of object relationships in both external and internal worlds. It is the mediator between needs and demand of inner world and realities and opportunities of outside, and as such has to pay heed to the superego

9.2.5.2. Superego

Superego is developed from ego. It is a part of the ego where self-observation and self-criticism occurs. It is roughly equivalent to a conscience (but not exactly; concerned with meta-psychology not ethics; has unconscious elements; derives from past so may conflict with present values).

It contains internal representations and standards of parental figures from early infancy onwards. It may manifest primitive punitive aspects as well as the more positive ego ideal.

9.2.5.3. Id

Id is the home of instinctual processes within a single person. It is disorganised as well as a passions. The ego and superego put much of their energy into managing id impulses.

9.2.5.4. Anxiety and Psychic Pain

Unacceptable aspects of mental processes may be rejected and forced into that area of experience called unconscious. This rejection may be motivated by, or may cause (if unconscious material threatens to become conscious) anxiety (response of ego to threat of sexual or aggressive drives, threat of loss, etc), depression, grief, etc.

Anxiety is a response to an as yet unrecognised factor; either environmental threat or repressed forces in self.

9.2.5.5. Developmental Phases

The way one handles basic drives and conflicts is determined in infancy by the responses of one's mother and significant others. There are biological and social phases that everyone goes through which provide a basic structure for incorporating later experience. Classical theory is tied to ideas about separation of ego and id so there is the need to postulate two parallel forms of development—libidinal and ego development.

9.3. Psychodynamic Psychotherapy

Psychodynamic psychotherapy is a method of verbal communication used to help a person find relief from emotional pain. It is based on the theories and techniques of psychoanalysis. Psychodynamic psychotherapy is similar to psychoanalysis in that it attributes emotional problems to the patient's unconscious motives and conflicts. It differs from classical psychoanalysis, however, in that psychodynamic psychotherapists do not necessarily accept Freud's view that these unconscious motives and conflicts are ultimately sexual in nature.

9.3.1. Objective of Psychodynamic Psychotherapy

Depending on the method of treatment, the goals of psychodynamic psychotherapy vary. Expressive therapy seeks to relieve symptoms through the development of insight, or the slowly developing awareness of feelings and thoughts that were once outside of the person's awareness.

Expressive therapy is based on the rationale that difficulties experienced in adult life originate in childhood; that children do not possess the maturity for making effective choices nor the independence to do so; and that methods of adapting that were developed in childhood may no longer be effective for adapting to the world as an adult. Through guidance from a therapist, the adult becomes aware of present ways of coping that are ineffective and how they served a purpose in childhood that is no longer relevant. The person learns that he or she now has a range of new options for solving problems, and for living in general that are now based on his or her maturity and independence.

Supportive therapy remains closer to the surface of the patient's issues. It is an approach that is used to relieve immediate distress; to return the person to his or her previous level of functioning; and to strengthen adaptive ways of coping that the individual already possesses in order to prevent further discomfort. Expressive and supportive methods of treatment are not completely separate categories because elements of supportive therapy are used in expressive treatment and vice versa, depending on the therapeutic need.

Psychotherapy alone is an effective method for treating mental disorders. However, some additional therapies as family therapy, couples therapy, or group therapy also make avail of individual treatment. A second treatment modality might be recommended when the patient's progress in individual treatment is highly dependent on relationships with significant others or with interpersonal relationships in general. Psychotropic (mood- or behaviour-altering) medication may also be prescribed as an adjunct (help) to treatment in order to manage disturbances in anxiety level, mood or thinking. Whether additional treatments are recommended is based on the needs of the individual.

Psychodynamic psychotherapy is very effective for treating prolonged sadness, anxiety, sexual difficulties, physical symptoms without physical basis, persistent feelings of isolation and loneliness, and the desire to be more successful in work or love. People seek therapy because they have not been able to develop a stable resolution for their difficulties on their own or with the help of friends and family members.

9.3.2. Methods of Treatment

While a client discusses the problem he is facing, the therapist gets the opportunity to learn about the person. It will further help him to develop an understanding of the client's troubles, and to formulate ideas about how treatment should proceed. This phase of interviewing and learning may take place in one session or over a series of sessions; or it may be done in a less structured manner, depending on the therapist's style. During the initial sessions, such factors as the frequency and length of sessions and the policy for payment will also be discussed.

After a certain period, the therapist and the individual will come to a mutual understanding of the goals for treatment. After this point, the sessions will become less like an interview; the person is asked to say whatever is on his or her mind. It is the therapist's job to listen and to help identify patterns of thinking, feeling and interacting that may be contributing to the patient's current struggles.

Consequently, the person becomes more aware of his or her thoughts and feelings; learns how some present ways of coping are no longer adaptive even though they may have been necessary in childhood; and discovers that he or she as an adult has a greatly expanded repertoire of resources and can use far more effective ways of dealing with problems. Deeper awareness and new insights stimulate psychological growth and change.

Psychodynamic psychotherapy places great importance on the therapeutic dyad, which is a medical term for the relationship between the therapist and the patient. It is within the context of the therapeutic dyad that positive changes in the patient's outlook and behaviors are able to unfold. This relationship is unique because the therapist maintains a uniform, neutral and accepting stance. Unlike other well-intentioned people in the person's life, the therapist has been trained to listen objectively and without criticism. This therapeutic attitude makes it easier for the person seeking treatment to speak freely and to therefore provide as much information for the thera ist to work with as is possible.

Treatment continues until the troubling symptoms have been reduced or alleviated and the person is consistently making use of more adaptive methods of coping with greater insight. For some people, this positive experience inspires them to proceed with further treatment in order to bring about additional adaptive changes. For others, meeting the initial goals will be sufficient. If so, the focus of sessions turns to issues related to the end of treatment.

The final phase of treatment is as important as the beginning and middle stages because it allows the individual to develop insight about his or her therapeutic experience. People need time to clarify how they feel about leaving the therapeutic relationship, and this termination involves identifying and understanding feelings about separation, maturation, loss and change. The length of time allotted to the termination phase varies with the type of treatment and with the needs of the individual.

9.3.3. Acceptance of the Therapy

Psychodynamic therapy is very effective for treating certain conditions like depression. But it is very difficult to measure the level of cure. The therapy evolves mixed response among the people. Psychodynamic therapy is one of the few mainstream therapies that focusses on aspects of your personality, and although it is used to treat a wide variety of conditions, it seems to us particularly suited for problems to do with personalities, and past and present relationships.

A person continues to handle difficulties in a more adaptive manner; experience improved interpersonal relationships and productivity at work; and continue to develop new insights into his or her thoughts, feelings and behaviour after certain period of treatment. In supportive treatment, insight and personality change are not the primary goals of treatment; the therapist and patient work toward a continuation of general stability in the person's life.

9.4. Conclusion

Life is very intricate and the travel of mind is very difficult to predict. Once the mind deviates from its path, it needs some treatment for recuperation. Human mind may be influenced by some external and internal factors. Whatever may be the cause of disorder, the illness should be treated in time.

References

Balsam, Rosemary Marshall, M.D., and Alan Balsam, M.D., *Becoming a Psychotherapist*, Chicago: The University of Chicago Press, 1984.

Dewald, Paul, M.D., "The Psychoanalytic Psychotherapies." In *Textbook of Psychoanalysis*, edited by Edward Nersessian, M.D. and Richard G. Kopff, M.D. Washington, DC: American Psychiatric Press, 1996.

Prochaska, James O., and John C. Norcross, *Systems of Psychotherapy: A Transtheoretical Analysis*, 4th edition, Pacific Grove: Brooks/Cole Publishing Company, 1999.

10

Rational Emotive Behaviour Therapy

10.1. Introduction

The overall wellbeing of a person depends on his physical as well as mental health. When the health of a person deflates, it will overturn not only his life but the people related to that person as well. Thoughts are the major contributor of a person's mental health. If one's thought is wretched, it will adversely affect his life. So, rational emotive behaviour therapy (REBT) focuses on uncovering irrational beliefs which may lead to unhealthy negative emotions and replacing them with more productive rational alternatives.

REBT is a comprehensive, active-directive, philosophically and empirically based psychotherapy which focuses on resolving emotional and behavioural problems and disturbances and enabling people to lead happier and more fulfilling lives. The positive thoughts lead a person into prosperity and happiness. Rational emotive behaviour therapy views human beings as 'responsibly hedonistic' in the sense that they strive to remain alive and to achieve some degree of happiness. However, it also holds that humans are prone to adopting irrational beliefs and behaviours which stand in the way of their achieving their goals and purposes. Often, these irrational attitudes or philosophies take the form of extreme or dogmatic 'musts', 'shoulds', or 'oughts'; they contrast with rational and flexible desires, wishes, preferences and wants.

The presence of extreme philosophies can make all the difference between healthy negative emotions (such as sadness or regret or concern) and unhealthy negative emotions (such as depression or guilt or anxiety). REBT maintains that individuals have it within their power to change their beliefs and philosophies profoundly, and thereby to change radically their state of psychological health.

10.2. Origin of REBT

REBT was created and developed by the American psychotherapist and psychologist Albert Ellis who was inspired by many of the teachings of Asian, Greek, Roman and modern philosophers. REBT is one of the first and foremost forms of Cognitive Behaviour Therapy (CBT) and was first expounded by Ellis in the mid-1950s.

People in most cases do not merely get upset by unfortunate adversities, but also through how they construct their view of reality through their evaluative beliefs and philosophies about these adversities. In REBT therapy clients usually learn and begin to apply this premise by learning the A-B-C-model of psychological disturbance and change. The A-B-C model first states that it normally is not merely A, adversities (or activating events) that lead to a disturbed and dysfunctional emotional and behavioural consequences—at C, but adversity times what people B, believe (peoples belief system) in relation to the these event. This belief system is highly evaluative and consists of interrelated cognitive, emotional and behavioural aspects.

To understand the role of their mediating evaluative and philosophically based irrational and self-defeating beliefs in upset, clients often can learn to identify them, begin to D, dispute, challenge and question them and come up with more rational and functional ones for then to subsequently begin to experience relief from their self-defeating emotions and behaviours.

Humans have both innate rational, meaning self- and social-helping and constructive, and irrational, meaning self- and social-defeating and un-helpful tendencies. People to a large degree create and construct emotional difficulties such as self-blame, self-pity, clinical anger, hurt, guilt, shame, depression and anxiety, and behaviours and behaviour tendencies like procrastination, over-compulsiveness, avoidance, addiction and withdrawal by the means of their irrational and self-defeating thinking, emoting and behaving.

In REBT, the therapist often teaches the client how to identify irrational and self-defeating beliefs which in nature are rigid, extreme, unrealistic, illogical and absolutist, and then to forcefully and actively dispute them and replace them with more rational and self-helping ones. By using different cognitive, emotive and behavioural methods and activities, the client, together with help from the therapist and in homework exercises, can gain a more rational, self-helping and constructive rational way of thinking, emoting and behaving.

10.3. Objectives of REBT

The prime objective of REBT is to show the client that whenever unpleasant activating events occur in people's lives, they have a choice of making themselves feel healthily and self-helpingly sorry, disappointed, frustrated, and annoyed, or making themselves feel unhealthily and self-defeatingly horrified, terrified, panicked, depressed, self-hating, and self-pitying. By attaining a more rational and self-constructive philosophy of themselves, others and the world, people often are more likely to behave and emote in a more life-serving and adaptive ways.

Ellis' first insight describes that mostly, people accepting the reality because their emotional disturbances at point C do not stem from the activating events or adversities at point A that precede C. Although A contributes to C, and although strong negative A's (such as being assaulted or raped) are much more likely to be followed by disturbed C's (such as feelings of panic and depression) than they are to be followed by weak A's (such as being disliked by a stranger), the main or more direct cores of emotional disturbances (C's) are people's irrational beliefs-the absolutistic musts and their accompanying inferences and attributions that people strongly believe about their undesirable activating events.

Secondly, people's acquisition of self-defeating, irrational beliefs mainly leads to their dysfunctional, emotional-behavioural consequences. If they are disturbed today, they tend to keep holding these irrational beliefs and upsetting themselves by them not because they held them in the past but because they are still actively, though often unconsciously, reaffirming them and acting as if they are still valid. They still follow, in their minds and in their hearts, the core masturbatory philosophies that they may have taken over or invented years ago, or that they have more recently accepted or constructed for themselves.

Thirdly, insight alone will rarely enable people to undo their emotional disturbances. They may feel better when they know, or think they know, how they became disturbed and are still making themselves upset largely because they believe these insights to be useful and curative.

There is usually no way but work and practice to keep looking for and finding one's core irrational beliefs; to actively, energetically, and scientifically dispute them; to replace one's absolutist musts with flexible preferences; to change one's unhealthy feelings to healthy, self-helping emotions; and to firmly act against one's dysfunctional fears and compulsions. Only by a combined cognitive, emotive, and behavioural, as well as a quite persistent and forceful, attack on one's serious emotional problems is one likely to significantly ameliorate or remove them-and keep them removed.

10.3.1. Evaluation of the Theory

Human thinking, emotion, and action are not really separate or disparate processes but that they all significantly overlap and are rarely experienced in a pure state. Much of what we call emotion is nothing more nor less than a certain kind-a biased, prejudiced, or strongly evaluative kind-of thought. But emotions and behaviours significantly influence and affect thinking, just as thinking.

Evaluating is a fundamental characteristic of human organisms and seems to work in a kind of closed circuit with a feedback mechanism. Because perception biases response and then response tends to subsequent perception. Also, prior perceptions appear to bias subsequent perceptions, and prior responses to bias subsequent responses. What we call feelings almost always have a pronounced evaluating or appraisal element.

People are born and reared with the ability to look at the data of their lives, particularly the negative things that happen to them against their goals and interests, and to make inaccurate inferences and attributions about these data. REBT differs from psychoanalysis in that it places little emphasis on exploring the past, but instead focuses on changing the current evaluations and philosophical thinking about people's lives, others and themselves.

10.3.2. Psychological Dysfunction

REBT rests on the pillar that irrational patterns of thinking, feeling and behaving are the cause of much, though hardly all, human disturbance. REBT teaches that when people turn flexible preferences, desires and wishes into grandiose absolutistic Jehovah demands and commands, they disturb and upset themselves.

10.3.2.1. Beliefs Disturbance

Some people believe that they must always perform well under all conditions. A deviation from this is unthinkable for them. If they fail, they feel bad, incompetent, unworthy and they think they always fail and deserve to suffer. This belief usually contributes to feelings of anxiety, panic, depression, despair, and worthlessness.

Some may have the opinion that they should be treated nicely in all circumstances. If they fail to get such recognition, they think that others are rotten, bad, unworthy people. This belief usually contributes to feelings of anger, rage, fury, and vindictiveness and lead to actions like fights, feuds, wars, genocide, and perhaps ultimately an atomic holocaust.

Some thinks that the conditions they live must be favourable, safe, hassle-free, and quickly and easily enjoyable. Whenever it disturbs, they think that their life is impossible and hardly worth living. This beliefs usually contributes to frustration and discomfort, intolerance, self-pity, anger, depression, and to behaviours such as procrastination, avoidance, and inaction.

At the core of irrational beliefs there often is an explicit or implicit rigid demand and command, and that extreme derivatives like awfulising, low frustration tolerance, people deprecation and over-generalisations are accompanied by these. A key tenet in the REBT framework is that the evaluative belief system, based on core philosophies, is very likely to create unrealistic, arbitrary, and crooked inferences and distortions in thinking.

REBT holds the devoutly held absolutistic philosophies and beliefs often contribute to disturbances, and that these inflexible and self-defeating philosophies are better replaced with more flexible, self-constructive and self-helping attitudes. The wrong evaluations generally occur through over-generalisation, wherein people exaggerate and globalise events or traits, usually unwanted events or traits or behaviour, out of context, while almost always ignoring the positive events or traits or behaviours.

Awfulising is mental magnification of the importance of an unwanted situation to a catastrophe, elevating the rating of something from bad to worse than it should be, to beyond totally bad, worse than bad to the intolerable and to a holocaust. The same exaggeration and over generalising occurs with human rating, wherein humans come to be defined by their flaws or misdeeds: the person is bad based on bad behaviour or bad traits. Frustration intolerance occurs when one perceive something to be too difficult, painful or tedious, and by doing so exaggerates these qualities beyond ones ability to cope with them.

REBT argues that mental wellness results from a surfeit of rational and self-helping ways of thinking, emoting and behaving. When an undesired and stressful activating event occurs, and the individual is interpreting, reacting to and evaluating the situation rationally and self-helpingly, then the resulting consequence is likely to be more healthy, constructive and functional. This does not mean a relatively undisturbed person never experiences negative feelings, but REBT does hope to keep debilitating unhealthy affect and behaviour to a minimum. To do this REBT promotes a flexible, un-dogmatic, self-helping and efficient belief system and constructive philosophy about adversities.

People in addition to disturbing themselves, also are innately constructivists. Because they largely upset themselves with their beliefs, they can be helped to examine, to question, to think about these beliefs and thereby to develop a more workable, more self-helping set of constructs.

10.4. REBT Therapy

According to Albert Ellis, "Humans, unlike just about all the other animals on earth, create fairly sophisticated languages which not only enable them to think about their feeling, and their actions, and the results they get from doing and not doing certain things, but they also are able to think about their thinking and even think about thinking about their thinking." This is quite essential to the REBT thought. He further added that "because of their self-consciousness and their ability to think about their thinking, they can very easily disturb themselves about their disturbances and can also disturb themselves about their ineffective attempts to overcome their emotional disturbances." In REBT terminology, this is referred to as secondary disturbances.

Forceful and active disputing is one of the most popular methods in REBT. It helps the client challenge and question irrational and self-defeating beliefs. These disputing processes incorporate cognitive-philosophic, emotive-evocative-dramatic, and behavioural methods necessary to successfully challenge the irrational beliefs. In therapy the therapist may point out irrational and self-defeating beliefs, but he or she also teaches the client how to dispute them in day-to-day life outside of therapy and also gives the patient homework exercises. The result of disputing the self-defeating belief and replacing it with a rational one yields an effective new philosophy.

By using emotive, cognitive and behavioural methods the client learns effective ways to dispute, question and replace the irrational and self-defeating beliefs with more rational and self-constructive ones, which then are likely to cause and create healthier and more constructive emotions and behaviour. The therapist is most interested in finding core beliefs and deep rooted philosophical evaluations. These contribute to automatic negative inferences and higher level cognitions.

As per REBT, understanding and insight are not enough. In order for clients to significantly change, they had better pinpoint their irrational philosophies and work forcefully and actively at changing them to more functional and self-helping attitudes. Although REBT teaches that the therapist had better demonstrate unconditional other-acceptance, the therapist is not necessarily always encouraged to build a warm and caring relationship with the client. The therapist's most important task is to aid the client in identifying and confronting irrational thinking, emotive, and behavioural processes and through a manner of ways and methodologies replace them with more rational ones.

The client has to work hard to get better, and this work may include homework assigned by the therapist. The assignments may for example include desensitisation tasks, i.e., by having the client confront the very thing he or she is afraid of. By doing so, the client is actively acting against the belief which often is contributing greatly to his disturbance.

The focus of REBT is on specific problems and is used as a brief therapy, but in deeper and more complex problems longer therapy is promoted. Another factor contributing to the brevity of REBT is that the therapist helps the client learn how to get better through hard work, and to help himself get through future adversities. It holds that hard work, and hard work only, is the way to get better and to stay that way.

REBT does rarely promote any temporary solutions. An ideal successful collaboration between the REBT therapist and a client results in changes to the client's philosophical way of evaluating him- or herself, others, and his or her life, and which is likely to yield effective results: The client moves toward unconditional self-acceptance, other-acceptance, and life-acceptance.

10.4.1. Remedial Approach of REBT

The objective behind the development of REBT is for helping clients to replace absolutist philosophies, full of 'musts' and 'shoulds', with more flexible ones; part of this includes learning to accept that all human beings are fallible and learning to increase their tolerance for frustration while aiming to achieve their goals. Although emphasising the same 'core conditions' as person-centred counselling—namely, empathy, unconditional positive regard, and counsellor genuineness—in the counselling relationship, REBT views these conditions as neither necessary nor sufficient for therapeutic change to occur.

In the beginning of REBT, the client acknowledges the existence of a problem and identifying any 'meta-disturbances' about that problem. He then identifies the underlying irrational belief which caused the original problem and comes to understand both why it is irrational and why a rational alternative would be preferable. The client challenges their irrational belief and employs a variety of cognitive, behavioural, emotive and imagery techniques to strengthen their conviction in a rational alternative. They identify impediments to progress and overcome them, and they work continuously to consolidate their gains and to prevent relapse.

REBT advocates 'selective eclecticism', which means that REBT counsellors are encouraged to make use of techniques from other approaches, while still working specifically within the theoretical framework of REBT. In other words, REBT maintains theoretical coherence while pragmatically employing techniques that work.

Throughout, the counsellor may take a very directive role, actively disputing the client's irrational beliefs, agreeing homework assignments which help the client to overcome their irrational beliefs, and in general 'pushing' the client to challenge themselves and to accept the discomfort which may accompany the change process.

10.5. Criticisms

REBT is easy to practice poorly. This may inspire wrong persons to practice it. The kind of conceptual disputing favoured by REBT could easily meander off track into minutiae relatively far removed from the client's central concern, and the mental gymnastics required to keep client and therapist on the same track could easily eat up time better spent on more productive activities. The counsellor's and client's estimations of relative importance could diverge rather profoundly, particularly if the client's outlook really does embody significant irrationalities. Having said all that, each of the preceding sentences includes the qualifier 'could', and with a great deal of skill, each pitfall undoubtedly could be avoided.

The need to match therapeutic approach with client preference is even more pressing with REBT than with many others. In other words, it seems very important to adopt the REBT approach only with clients who truly are suitable, as it otherwise risks being strongly counter-productive. On this point, however, it is crucial to realise that some clients specifically do appreciate exactly this kind of approach, and counsellors who are unable or unwilling to provide the disputation required are probably not right for those clients.

10.6. Conclusion

Life is meaningful when it is led by positive attitudes. For this, people should realise their positive and negative qualities and behave accordingly. REBT empowers persons with unconditional self-acceptance, other-acceptance, life-acceptance are of prime importance in achieving mental wellness. Relaxation in life is essential for setting aside unwanted thoughts. REBT upholds the ideas and feelings about self-worth are largely definitional and are not empirically confirmable.

References

Ellis, Albert, *Feeling better, getting better, staying better*, New York: Impact Publishers, 2001.

________________, *Overcoming Destructive Beliefs, Feelings, and Behaviours: New Directions for Rational Emotive Behaviour Therapy*, Prometheus Books, 2001.

________________, "Early theories and practices of rational emotive behaviour theory and how they have been augmented and revised during the last three decades", *Journal of Rational-Emotive & Cognitive-Behaviour Therapy*, 2003.

Ellis, Albert, Mike Abrams and Lidia Abrams, *Personality Theories: Critical Perspectives*, New York: Sage Press, 2008.

Froggatt, Wayne, *A Brief Introduction To Rational Emotive Behaviour Therapy*, Third Edition, New Zealand Centre for Cognitive Behaviour Therapy, 2005.

11

Counselling and Psychotherapy with Children and Adolescents

11.1. Introduction

Childhood is the most happiest period in one's life. It is a period for playing, merrymaking, learning, etc. It is a tension free life. No responsibility except learning. But, today, the competitiveness around the world engulfs the childhood also. They are also passing through mental tortures and tensions. For scoring high percentage marks, or winning co-curricular activities, they are suffered heavy burdens. The psychological treatment of children's problems is the focus of several professions and is carried out in many settings and situations. Although theoretical viewpoints are wide-ranging and essentially rooted in adult-based theories, the child or adolescent presents a unique challenge to the child mental health worker.

11.2. Mental Health Needs of Children and Adolescents

The mental set up of children is totally different from that of adults. Their treatment cannot be viewed as scaled-down adult therapy; their developmental stages, environments, reasons for entering therapy, and other relevant factors necessitate a different, if not creative, approach to therapy. The child/adolescent therapist must have an expanded knowledge base of the human condition and a different perspective of what constitutes therapy or counselling.

Childhood, the most beautiful period in life, sometimes changed into a den of miseries for some children. They expect caring care, love, affection and recognition from their parents and other family members. But, in a busy life schedule, the parents may not get quality time to spend with their children. This may make them alone and mentally unsafe, and it will ultimately leads to mental disorders.

Melanie Klein, emphasising the symbolic importance of children's play, introduced free play with children as a substitute for the free association technique used with adults, thus inventing play therapy. Although these two camps disagreed on many issues, they have remained the dominant voices in the child psychoanalytic field, with most analytic work being a spin-off of either Freud or Klein.

The mental health treatment of children and adolescents has also been affected by two policy and legislative mandates. First, the community mental health movement was strongly influenced by the passage in 1963 of the federal programme to construct mental health centers in local communities and begin a move away from large institutional treatment. This movement grew not only because it was mandated by a federal programme but because it represented a philosophy that mental health interventions are more likely to be successful when carried out in the community where the maladjustment is occurring. The new programmes emphasised early intervention and prevention of mental disorders. The second mandate, with a similar philosophical base, involved the provision of special education services to all handicapped children, including emotionally disturbed and behaviour-disordered children and adolescents.

Psychotherapy and mental health treatment, if deemed a part of the total educational program of a child, has become by law and policy an educational service. The most recent movement in child and adolescent treatment has been in the identification of treatments that are evidence based. Various terms have been used to describe these treatments including empirically validated or supported treatments, evidence-based practice, or simply treatments that work.

Efforts have also been made to quantify the degree and strength of support for the treatments, for example, the number of studies showing evidence of effectiveness. Studies are examined with the specification of treatment (i.e., age, setting, presenting problem), use of treatment manuals or clearly specified intervention procedures, and evaluation of outcome with multiple measures. Procedures must be replicable and independent replication studies are often included in criteria for a treatment to be labelled as evidence based.

Children and adolescents remain critically underserved populations, despite ample recognition of the problem based on nearly 40 years of research documenting needs. The mental health needs of children present an enormous service delivery shortfall; and with funding problems continuing in the human services, the gap between need and available services is likely to continue. Preventive services may be a cost- and resource-efficient mode for dealing with part of this problem, but the provision of quality counselling and psychotherapeutic services will be a crucial component in the total mental health system.

The complex needs of children and adolescents, including:

- Development of comprehensive home- and community-based services and supports.
- Development of family support and partnerships.
- Development of culturally competent care and reducing disparities in access to care.
- Individualisation of care.
- Implementation of evidence-based practice.
- Service coordination and designation responsibility.
- Prevention activities for at-risk groups with earlier identification and intervention, including programs for early childhood.
- Expansion of mental health services in the schools.

Healthy mind leads to healthy citizens and it will ultimately leads to development. Mental health is very important for the economical development of a nation. The child/adolescent mental health worker must be familiar with human development for a number of reasons. With the exception of severe psychopathology or extreme behaviours, much of what is presented as problematic in children may simply be normal developmental deviation.

Children observe things differently. For them, everything has theirown explanation. Knowledge of development and the normal behavioural ranges at different ages is crucial to discriminating between truly deviant behaviour and minor developmental crises. Development in children and adolescents may follow sequences with expected orders for the appearance of certain behaviours and characteristics yet still tend to be highly variable.

11.3. Psychological Issues in Children and Adolescents

Besides developmental issues, a number of other issues related to the child's development and situation have an impact on the psychotherapeutic relationship. These factors relate to the direct work with the child or adolescent and stem from some of the differences between child/adolescent psychotherapy and adult psychotherapy.

The major threat before a therapist while treating a child or adolescent patient is that they are not ready to accept they have a problem. Instead they believe that they are completely right and the others are completely wrong. The child is unlikely to voluntarily initiate entering into therapy. This decision is usually made by an adult in the child's environment, with some varying degree of acceptance/compliance/ resistance from the child. The involuntary nature of the child/adolescent client in many cases may yield little or no motivation on the part of the client to engage in a relationship with the therapist or not even an admission that any change is necessary. Thus, the first step in many interventions may be simply to establish some type of relationship with the child and to come to some agreement that change is necessary.

The child/adolescents lack understanding of both the therapeutic process and the treatment objectives. The adult is likely to recognise the need to "get something out of therapy" and to have certain expectations of what is supposed to happen in the counselling situation. The adult usually will be able to verbalise some expectations and goals and to engage in some role-appropriate "client behaviours."

The child may not have clear view of what the therapy situation presents. This blurred view may range from having total disinformation to seeing the therapist as an agent of his or her parents, the school, the courts, or some other individual or institution that forced the initiation of treatment. The therapist may initially have to simply educate the child about therapy, explaining what it is and what it is not. Children may bring in distorted or stereotyped perceptions of therapists.

The goals, objectives, and topics or content for the counselling should also be revealed before a child/adolescent client. The therapist needs to demonstrate to the child or adolescent client that the client will get something out of counselling. Initially, this demonstration may take a form as simple as providing an interesting format. This accomplishment can lead to the establishment of a more congruent set of objectives.

11.3.1. Limitations of Child in Conveying Emotions

Moreover, the child has more limited verbal and linguistic development. Children may be unable to think in more abstract terms and may have even more difficulty verbally describing and discussing their thoughts and emotions. This limited verbal ability is one of the main reasons play has been used as a medium of therapy. Play and other nonverbal techniques allow expression without creating anxiety or frustration for the child because of an inability to find the correct verbal description.

Children also differ from adults in terms of their dependence on environmental forces and changes. Children are reactors to changes in their living situations rather than initiators of change. They have relatively little power to take action to eliminate or prevent environmental causes of stress. They react to parental divorces, family moves, and school and peer pressures. The child's disturbance may actually be a relatively normal reaction to upheaval or stress in the environment.

Even if the child makes significant progress in individual therapy, he or she still does not have the options available to adults in dealing with the environment. In some cases, therapy may even proceed on the notion of helping the child cope with a stressful situation, rather than assuming that change will be forthcoming in the environment.

The child has a greater range of normal emotional and behavioural responses as a result of the unformed nature of the personality. The therapist, therefore, can be more flexible and must anticipate and not be discouraged by seemingly broad swings of emotion and behaviour in the course of treatment. The plasticity of the child's personality is also an asset in the working out of a preventive model that heads off disturbing patterns with appropriate intervention prior to the crystallisation of the personality.

11.3.2. Mental Disorders in Children

Childhood is also a period of inculcating values and thereby formulating personality. The other child development information relevant to the child/adolescent therapist comes from the study of personality factors that are essentially specific developmental variables. In many cases, these factors are components of the major personality theories.

Dependency, anxiety and insecurity, aggressiveness, and achievement motivation are the factors commonly involved in child and adolescent problems. In looking at each factor, we find a developmental pattern, behavioural manifestations, contributing factors to problematic instances of the factor, and adaptive and maladaptive outcomes. Dependency may involve child-adult relationships in which the child is often seeking help and physical contact, engaging in attention-seeking behaviour, and maintaining physical proximity to the adult. These behaviours are relatively normal and expected with young children and their parents. As children get older, both the intensity of the dependency and the object of emotional dependence change.

When a child grows, they become less dependent on their parents, with a resulting decrease in the dependent behaviours, and become more dependent on peers for approval and attention. Certain parental patterns are seen as contributing to a child's overdependence and interfering with the move toward greater independence. The child who makes adequate progress in this area develops a sense of trust, is responsive to social reinforcers, and is able to display warmth toward others. The overly dependent child is more likely to become a passively dependent individual, submissive, and mistrusting of others.

For dependency and other personality factors, a normal developmental progression is viewed as important to successful adult adjustment. Knowledge of these variables can be used in treatment planning and goal setting, in determining whether excessive or pathological behaviours are occurring at different ages, and in assessing contributing factors to problematic behaviours.

11.3.3. Period of Teenage

Adolescence is a phase which comprised of full of curiosity as well as tensions. In teenage, they may think that all that glitters is gild. This period provides a tough time for parents and teachers. Probably no single developmental period provides more confusion and consternation for parents, teachers, and clinicians than adolescence. The uniqueness of adolescence has long been recognised as a key crossroads in human development. They are making the transition from childhood to adulthood.

Normal adolescent development will be characterised by a range of distressing, turbulent, and unpredictable thoughts, feelings, and actions and that, as a consequence of such storm and stress, adolescents will normatively display symptoms that in an adult would suggest definitive psychopathology. The adolescent therapist must be cautious not to over interpret typical and, perhaps, seemingly bizarre behaviour, thoughts, or feelings as indicating severe psychopathology. At the same time, the therapist should not be surprised or upset by a rocky, unpredictable, and frustrating course of treatment.

11.3.4. Problems among the Youth

The adolescence mostly lives in fantasy instead of reality. It is a phase for exploring new frontiers. In this period, the youths give more importance to their own self. In this period, the teenagers wish to get a life free from all kinds of limitations. They struggle to be independent and free from parental supervision and consent.

Adolescent is a period, where they create their on theories and laws by obfuscating the existing ones. They like to see the world on their own viewpoint. They are extremely interested in sexual matters, with initial heterosexual relationships often intense and over-idealised. The adolescent may become overconcerned with appearance and dress, spending considerable time preening and grooming.

The adolescent, as part of the struggle for independence, shifts his or her identity patterns from parents and family to a chosen peer group. The behaviours and characteristics, often shown through dress and other interests, usually are antithetical to and criticised by the adults from whom the adolescent is attempting to become independent. All is possible in adolescence. They also tend to display certain characteristic affective states and behaviours. They takes life intensely and passionately, sometimes overreacting. Minor concerns can become major issues, with the adolescent being indifferent to very little.

This period is also prone to sudden emotional reactions of joy and sadness. The shifts in affect are quick and intense. Rebelliousness may be common, and in some extreme cases delinquency and other antisocial behaviour may occur. The adolescent may have episodes of inhibition and may withdraw socially at times.

The period of adolescence is very delicate. Unless handle carefully, it leads to big troubles. The child/adolescent therapist will find much in theory and research in child and adolescent development that pertains to psychological interventions with these groups.

It is difficult to imagine developing and carrying out treatment plans without a firm grounding in these areas. Developmental theory and broader contextual perspectives provide us with a framework to systematically, if not scientifically, work with children and adolescents and more objectively gauge our therapeutic progress with them.

11.4. Difference in Treating Adult and Children

Children'may give more importance what the adults consider the most trivial. Children's personalities are quite unstable when compared with expectations of stability in adults. Related to this instability is the evidence that indicates normal development is often marked by a number of behaviour problems. The child/adolescent therapist must be able to sort out "normal" problems from those that may represent more serious disorders.

The therapists also be aware of the development. This awareness will also aid the therapist in clinical decision making at various points in the treatment process. Appropriate goal setting is important to any therapeutic venture. It provides a direction for our work, allows us to monitor progress, and tells us when we are done. The child/adolescent therapist sets these goals in a developmental framework and does not expect an average 8-year-old to acquire, in the course of therapy, the problem-solving cognitive abilities or the moral judgment of a 10-year-old.

For improving the mental health of children, the therapist first set up goals. This goals must not be above the developmental expectations, lest the intervention will fail. This knowledge of development also allows the therapist to choose appropriate content and to decide what level of therapeutic interaction is best suited for the child. Within these developmental age expectations, the therapist must also be sensitive to developmental delays in children. Delays, particularly in cognition and language, dictate goal setting, yet they must be distinguished from behavioural or emotional disorders. These delays may also be major contributing factors in the development of disorders.

Children with learning disabilities or mental retardation often display poor self-concepts and negative self-images as well as other socio-emotional difficulties. On the other end of the spectrum, we need to be cautious not to set limited goals for developmentally advanced children. Although we are not advocating psychological assessment as a prerequisite for treatment, in most cases, the child/adolescent therapist will need to assess developmental levels of their clients early in the intervention.

10.4.1. Piaget's Theory of Cognitive Development

Piaget's theory of cognitive development provides a parallel base for assessing intellectual development. Cognitive development is a coherent and fixed sequence with certain cognitive abilities expected at certain ages. Piaget allows us to select developmentally appropriate modes of interacting with the child and to set appropriate goals for cognitive change.

Morality has an important role in molding the behaviour of a child. Moral judgment is seen as a developmental, age-bound variable similar to the cognitive and psychosexual stages. At different ages, the individual has certain beliefs about the reasons for displaying moral behaviour, the value attached to a human life, and the reasons for conforming to moral standards.

Awareness of the stages of moral development can provide insights into the behaviour of the child, provide content for therapy sessions, and also allow therapy to be conducted at levels commensurate with current moral development levels.

Whenever the moral values show a sign of recession, it is related to child deviance, particularly delinquency. At each stage, the individual encounters a crisis that he or she must resolve by acquiring a new phase of social interaction. An unsuccessful resolution of a psychosocial crisis impedes further development and can have a negative effect on the individual's personality.

11.4.2. Psychotherapeutic Intervention with Adolescents

The behaviour of adolescents is unpredictable and a similar unpredictability exists in the therapeutic relationship. Psychotherapy with disturbed adolescents is a demanding task. Adolescents entering the therapy situation are characteristically impatient, intolerant, and uncommunicative. They may fail to elaborate on any details of the current situation or difficulties presented. They may deny any responsibility for the current problems, preferring to place blame elsewhere, or may actually have almost no insight into the reasons they have been referred for treatment.

The therapy is effective if there is a relation between the therapist and the client. Mostly, the therapist fail to make a healthy relationship with his adolescent client and it will leads to the failure of the therapy. Although the adolescent may be a difficult client, most disturbed adolescents are accessible to psychotherapeutic intervention. Depending on the level of development and maturity, work with the adolescent may range from game like approaches utilised with younger children to therapy that resembles interventions with an adult presenting similar problems.

While treating adolescents, the therapist must attempt to put the adolescent at ease, explaining what to expect and taking steps to suppress apprehensions. Unstructured probing, queries about deep personal feelings, or challenging the adolescent to explain his or her misbehaviour will likely produce further uncooperativeness or yield a strong emotional response.

Beginning with factual information in a nonjudgmental manner will help allay initial anxieties.

The therapist needs to explain how the relationship will differ from those with parents, teachers, peers, and others. The goal at this level is to achieve engagement with the adolescent and then implant the initial seeds for establishing a motivation. The initial agreement from the adolescent may simply be to return to another session.

The therapists must be ready to give their full attention to an adolescent client while treating. Long silences, noncommittal responses, and long periods of formulating answers to the adolescent's concerns should be avoided. Adolescent therapists may find they talk with these clients relatively more than with adult clients. Explaining thoughts explicitly, phrasing questions concretely, and, in general, using a direct approach will facilitate work with the adolescent.

11.4.3. Multisystemic Therapy and Role of Parents

Multisystemic therapy (MST) treatment was originally developed for interventions with antisocial and delinquent youth. The approach is based on social-ecological theory that includes treatment considerations at the individual, family, peer, school, and community levels. In this perspective, the individual child or adolescent is viewed as at the center of a variety of interacting and interdependent systems. Treatments aimed at these various systems can be done simultaneously and can ultimately impact the individual. All these levels are viewed as potentially contributing to the development of emotional and behavioural problems, as well as to the maintenance of the difficulties.

Education must be adequate for combating troubles in children and adolescents. Children need support from parents and teachers. Any deviation from this makes chaos. Parental interventions may involve parenting classes or perhaps therapy for the parents. In most cases, a multimodal, or combined, approach will be used.

A high school guidance counsellor may work individually with an adolescent whose family is in therapy with a licensed psychologist. A further assumption here is that a person does not have to be called a therapist to have therapeutic impact on a child. The second, related assumption involves the settings where treatment takes place. Troubled children and adolescents receive treatment in, among other places, classrooms, schools, agencies, clinics, group homes, and hospitals.

The problems before the child and adolescent are family problems, learning/underachievement, motivation/attitude, attention deficit /hyperactivity, and divorce. These problems have roots in the family and environment. These are very delicate issues and the psychologists must be extra careful while handling such problems.

11.5. Efficacy of the Treatment

Lack of proper guidance is the root cause of all types of mental illness. Values in life should be nurtured in the minds of people in their childhood. Parents and teachers should be well educated and broad-minded to see the depth of problems. They must possess knowledge about bringing up children. Unnecessary poured over the shoulders of children only help to aggravate the situation.

Medicines and counselling is meant for taking out the mental troubles. Psychotherapy represents a wide variety of techniques, in some ways preventing a clear, unambiguous definition of psychotherapy. Psychotherapy differs depending on the theoretical orientation of the therapist, the length of time of the treatment. The clinical definition of client populations may be ambiguous and thus limit generalisability.

The characteristics of therapists may also influence the rate of recovery. Therapists vary in age, sex, training, orientation, competency, style, and personality characteristics. Outcome could be affected by any one of these.

The character of children is influenced by his/her surroundings, the people they come in contact with, etc. Father, mother, siblings, friends and teachers, etc have a greater influence on children. The therapy works only when the client discloses their mental troubles to the therapist.

Problem-solving skills trainings has shown effectiveness with even fairly young children through adolescents. The basic tenet of problem-solving training involves recognition of the problems, generation of possible responses to the problems, and selection of a behaviour that is "good" for the situation. Often, teachers and parents are trained to facilitate this process with children. A variant of this has been shown to be effective in dealing specifically with anger issues in adolescents. This approach focuses more specifically on alternatives to aggression.

11.6. Conclusion

Love, caress, affection and recognition, etc are the priceless presents everybody craves for. The lack of such things makes problems at stages in life. The phase of childhood and adolescence is also not free from tensions and stresses. But, the psychological needs of children and adolescents are different. The mental health needs of children create enormous demands that the social services and mental health delivery system have not yet even closely met. The child/adolescent therapist must be aware of developmental factors and plan and conduct treatment accordingly. Further, the therapist must be aware of the unique aspects of the therapeutic relationship with children and adolescents. The complexities in life and the pressure for winning the top ranks also aggravate the situation. They have a delicate mind and while handling their problems, the therapist must be extra careful.

References

Abramowitz, C. V., "The effectiveness of group psychotherapy with children", *Archives of General Psychiatry*, 1980.

Axline, V., "Play therapy", Boston: Houghton Mifflin, 1947.

Barrett, C. L., Hampe, I. E., & Miller, L., "Research on psychotherapy with children", In S. L. Garfield & A. D. Springfield, 1978

Casey, R. J., & Berman, J. S., "The outcome of psychotherapy with children", *Psychological Bulletin*, 1985.

Christophersen, E. R., & Mortweet, S. L., "Treatments that work with children: Empirically supported strategies for managing childhood problems", Washington, DC: American Psychological Association, 2001.

Clarizio, H. F., & McCoy, G. F., *Behavior disorders in children* (3rd ed.), New York: HarperCollins, 1983.

Cramer-Azima, F. & Richmond, L.H. (ed), *Adolescent Group Psychotherapy (monograph)*, American Group Psychotherapy Association.

Erickson, M. T., *Behavior disorders of children and adolescents: Assessment, etilogy, and intervention,* (3rd ed.). Englewood Cliffs, NJ: Prentice-Hall, 1997.

Erikson, E. H., *Childhood and society* (2nd ed.), New York: Norton, 1963.

Malekoff, A., *Group Work with Adolescents, Principles and Practice,* N.Y., Guilford Press, 1997.

Rose, S.R., *Group Work with Children and Adolescents: Prevention and Intervention in School and Community System,* London, Sage Pub, 1998.

12

Ethics in Psychotherapy and Counselling

12.1. Introduction

Mind is a storing place for all secrets. Everybody likes to keep such secrets as secrets. But whenever we face some problems in life and unable to find a way out, we are forced to reveal these secrets to those we trust most. But the trust is just a belief. After all, all are human beings and are prone to illegal behaviours.

Psychotherapy is a treatment in which the therapists try to liberate the minds of their clients from the grip of unwanted thoughts and disorders. Therapists are the guides who change the life of their clients in a meaningful way. Through therapy, clients can find their strengths. They can confront loss, tragedy, hopelessness, and the end of life in ways that do not leave them numb or paralysed. They can discover what brings them joy and what sustains them in hard times. They can begin to trust, or to trust more wisely. They can learn new behaviours in therapy and how to teach themselves new behaviours after therapy ends. They can question what they always believed was unquestionable. They can find out what matters most to them and stop wasting time. They can become happier, or at least less miserable.

12.2. Role of the Therapist

Helping somebody when they are in need is the biggest thing we all can do. The world is in the turmoil of tensions and stresses. We all are guided by emotions, feelings, thoughts, desires, etc. When we fail, or fear to fail in our life, we feel insecure and confine in the formicary of despondence. This despondence may leads them to end their life or they may land in more sever problems.

Crime, cruelty, suicides, etc are the child of bad mind. When a person loses hopes, he may commit suicide. Marriage is a dignified relation and today, there are lots of loopholes in this relation also. If a spouse is not loyal and keeps a liaison relation with somebody, this may create endless problems in married life. Describing all such things may not be possible for everybody. We are ready to disclose our problems with those we trust.

People face a lot of problems in their day to day life. They may be minor, hard-to-define problems, yet the hard, risky, unpredictable twists and turns of their therapy can lead to more meaningful, effective, fulfilling lives. The therapists may respond differently with the clients. According to the nature of the therapist, some may respond lightly, some set aside their concern about a suicidal client between sessions. A few may sit unmoved while a client talks, perhaps for the first time, about what it was like to survive an atrocity while others may turn away untroubled when a managed care company refuses to authorise treatment for someone in desperate need of help.

The people who involved in the field of psychological therapies have a lot of responsibilities. They must realise these responsibilities and should decide how to respond to stressful and sometimes overwhelming. We may feel short of time, resources, or wisdom. The responsibilities can weigh us down, rattle us, make us want to run and hide. They can make us more vulnerable to other sources of stress.

Uncertainty causes stress for some of us. There is no reference book which helps us in crisis. Sometimes, we are unable to get guidance in the time of crisis. We are constantly thrown back on our own judgment. If we believe a client might kill someone but there is no explicit threat or other legal justification under the state's law to hospitalise the client or breach confidentiality, we become helpless.

12.2.1. Rational Thinking

The rational thinking of a therapist is very much important for treating mental illness. Sometimes, a therapist forced to take a decision with out the consent of his client. After all, the prime objective of a therapist must be the recovery of the patient.

The inescapable responsibility of making careful, informed professional judgments regarding issues of enormous complexity and potentially life-and-death implications can push even the most resourceful therapists to their limits. Fearing that formal review agencies will hold us accountable after the fact stresses and distresses some of us. Some agencies, such as local, state, and national professional ethics committees, focus specifically on the ethical aspects of our work. Others, such as state licensing boards and the civil courts, enforce professional standards of care that may reflect ethical responsibilities.

The prospect of review agencies second-guessing us with the benefit of hindsight can make difficult judgments a nightmare for some therapists. They may suffer a debilitating performance anxiety, dread going to work, and discover that the focus of their work has changed from helping people to avoiding a malpractice suit. Managed care has stressed some therapists.

12.2.2. Periodicity of the Treatment

The average number of sessions needed for each patient, must limit the total number of sessions to make a profit. Strict guidelines may limit how many sessions a therapist can provide. Therapists may feel pressure to terminate before the limit. Even if clinicians follow the agency's formal procedures, they may face charges before an ethics committee, licensing board, or malpractice court for patient abandonment, improper denial of treatment, or similar issues.

Therapists may fear not only that a formal review agency will sanction them but also that the limited sessions fall far short of what their clients need. Teaching or learning therapy can stress some of us. As supervisors, we may grow uncomfortable with how the supervisee responds to the client differently from how we would, with our responsibility to evaluate the supervisee's work, and with the demands of our role as teacher and mentor. As supervisees, we may doubt our ability to carry out clinical responsibilities, dread making mistakes, feel uneasy about differences in values or theoretical orientation between ourselves and our supervisor, and figure that if we are completely honest in describing to our supervisor what we actually thought, felt, and did with our clients, we might be advised to look for another line of work.

12.2.3. Major Situation

Like any other field, psychotherapy is also not free from malpractices. But it should be checked in due course otherwise it will eat away the entire process. Some therapist may totally blind while they face some unforeseen situations. Each therapist must have higher ethical values. The degradation of values will destruct the life of their clients for ever.

12.2.3.1. Life in Troubles

For some of us, life is a mystery. Sometimes, we are unable to find out the meaning of life. If we face grave problems in our life, we may become very depressed. During the treatment, if the client has any physical problems and if unnoticed it may lead to the client's death. Negligence in diagnosing is common in medical field. The therapist must take care of not only the mental health of his patients but their physical health also.

12.2.3.2. Wrong Decisions

Taking wrong decisions is also possible in a psychological treatment. The therapists prescribe treatment by evaluating the symptoms. But it may evolve only negative results. Treatment should be given only after finding out the problem. The clients may show multiple problems. Sometimes, client may unable to describe what is pestering them. In such cases, the therapist gives advice depending on his/her mental evaluation. So, for avoiding wrong results, the therapist must go through the problems of the clients thoroughly and he has the power to imagine consequence of his treatment.

12.2.3.3. Fatal Disease

People will never disclose some diseases like AIDS to others. Such cases are revealed to the person who is the most reliable for the client. The therapist has the duty to keep the secrets, whatever it may, as secrets. He must not, at any circumstances, reveal it to anybody. The revelation of such diseases will make the life of patients miserable. So, it is duty of the therapists to keep secrets.

12.2.3.4. Ability of the Therapist

Sometimes patients may be the complaint that the therapists are practising outside the areas of competence. If the therapist has no formal education or training and has no supervised experience in treating people, it will also affect the health of the patient adversely. The therapist must possess adequate knowledge about treating people with different cultures and beliefs.

12.2.3.5. High Fee Structure

Some therapists may ask a huge some of money for treating psychological problems. The treatments are also getting very costly. Charging a very high amount as consulting fee is against medical ethics. All have the right to get expert advice during illness. If the fee is beyond the reach of common people, it may become the cause of another mental disorder.

12.2.3.6. Preventing Clients from further Crimes

Some psychic people may make dangers to the society. While undergoing treatment, a therapist may get the hint of what the client is brooding in his mind. If those thoughts are danger to the society, the therapist should take adequate measures to prevent the patient from doing something wrong.

Formal mechanisms of accountability act to protect clients from unethical and potentially harmful practices, but may also increase the stress. Society may hold therapists accountable for predicting and preventing homicide. But accurately predicting whether someone will or will not kill seem to be beyond the capacity of mental health professionals or anyone else, for that matter. In the midst of all this responsibility, complexity, uncertainty, and stress, remaining alert to the ethical aspects of our work in a consistent and meaningful manner can seem overwhelming.

12.3. Ethics and Denial

When the stress overpowers, all of us are vulnerable to denial and other ways of dismissing, distorting, or discounting ethical questions. We all have our favoured ways of making uncomfortable ethical challenges disappear, perhaps by transforming them almost magically into something else, perhaps by attacking the client or colleague who raises the ethical question, perhaps by viewing ourselves as helpless, as compelled by necessity to act in a way that we suspect may be unethical.

Self assessment is a useful method to tackle stress in a certain level. Take a few minutes to conduct a private self-assessment of the degree to which these forms of ethical denial may have infiltrated your own practice as a therapist, counsellor, supervisor, or trainee.

Professional ethics involve acknowledging the reality and importance of the individuals whose lives we affect. They involve understanding the nature of the professional relationship and professional interventions and they involve affirming accountability for our behaviour. A moment of active and honest self-assessment can give us at least a general sense of how well we are accomplishing these tasks.

12.3.1. Fundamental Postulations

A person's shared vulnerability to stress, denial, and human imperfection can make recognising and meeting his ethical responsibilities hard, and yet he cannot spare himself from constant ethical challenges, from responsibility for how his choices help or hurt.

Ethical awareness is a continuous, active process that involves constant questioning. Fatigue, habits, stress, dogma, and routine can erode our personal responsiveness and our sense of personal responsibility. They can lull us into ethical sleep, putting us on automatic when we need to wake up to what we are missing. It is crucial to practice continued alertness to the ethical implications of what we do.

Awareness of the ethical standards and codes is crucial to competence in the area of ethics, but standards and codes cannot take the place of an active, deliberative, and creative approach to fulfilling our ethical responsibilities. They prompt, guide, and inform rather than preclude our ethical considerations. We cannot apply standards and codes in rote, unthinking manner.

All new clients, whatever may be the similarities to previous clients, is unique. Each situation is unique and changes over time. Standards and codes may identify some approaches as clearly unethical. They may identify significant ethical values and concerns, but they cannot tell us what form these values and concerns will take. They may set forth essential tasks, but they cannot tell us the best way to accomplish those tasks with a unique client facing unique problems.

Knowledge of the scientific and professional literature, the evolving research, and theory is crucial to competence in the area of ethics, but the claims and conclusions emerging in the literature can never be passively accepted and reflexively applied. A necessary response to published claims and conclusions is active, careful, informed, persistent, and comprehensive questioning.

The overwhelming majority of therapists and counsellors are conscientious, dedicated, caring individuals who are committed to ethical behaviour. But none of us is infallible. Whatever our experience, accomplishments, or wisdom, all of us can-and do-make mistakes, overlook something important, and reach conclusions that are wrong.

The therapists repeatedly encounter ethical dilemmas for which a clear ethical response is elusive. The therapist confronts needs that do not match resources; values and responsibilities that clash; situations whose meaning varies according to perspective and context; limits to our scientific understanding of conditions or interventions; our own feelings; or other reactions that seem to block or sidetrack an effective response. There is no legitimate way to avoid these struggles.

12.4. Conclusion

There are some unwritten laws prevailing in the field of psychotherapy, which should not be broken. Ethics has very important role in this field and the existence of the therapy itself depends on this ethics. The matters a therapist handle is the secrets, which may have the power to take the head of many. But, whatever may be it, if it is not dangerous to the society, it should not be disclosed. Moreover, the therapist must respect the feelings of the clients. Giving accepting respect is also important here.

References

Blum, S. R., "Ethical issues in managed mental health", In S. Feldman (Ed.), *Managed mental health services,* Springfield, IL: Charles C. Thomas, 1992.

Geraty, R. D., Hendren, R. L., & Flaa, C. J., "Ethical perspectives on managed care as it relates to child and adolescent psychiatry", *Journal of the American Academy of Child and Adolescent Psychiatry*, 1992.

Olsen, D. P., "The ethical considerations of managed care in mental health treatment", *Journal of Psychosocial Nursing*, 1994.

Simon, N. P., "Practitioner ethics and managed care", *Managed Care Quarterly*, 1994.

Wineburgh, M., "Ethics, managed care, and outpatient psychotherapy", *Clinical Social Work Journal*, 1998.

13

Family Counselling and Psychotherapy

13.1. Introduction

Family is the primary institute of every people from where they learn the values of life. If the family of a person is not good, its traces will reflect in his character also. For the making of good and quality citizens, good family set up is essential. In such a way, if a person shows psychological problems, it will affect the entire family. Therefore, any psychological distress felt by an individual has roots in society at large.

The social set up prevailing in a nation also offers ample opportunity for psychological distress. Ever since the 19th century, traditional pre-industrial family values have been pushed aside in favour of the various pleasures of mass consumption. In a permissive, self-indulgent society, there is less and less use for self-discipline and self-restraint. When anything goes, nothing means anything, and all paths lead nowhere. And right in the middle of nowhere you are sure to find anxiety, depression, and distress.

However, all psychological problems can not be solved by changing society. Some political groups may try to suggest such .. solution, but ultimately the individual must be responsible for recognising and transcending-or "seeing through"-all the social illusions that can lead a person astray. Many persons have been brought to disaster by believing that they can change, control, or be responsible for anyone else.

Any attempt to control the thoughts or behaviour of another person is just an unconscious attempt to control-rather than face up to and heal-your own "ugly" inner life. And until you have made peace with yourself, you will never be able to live in peace with anyone else. So in this world you can't change anyone but yourself. Then, it can be hoped, your example might influence others to change themselves.

Different people have different concepts on life. It is true among the family members also. So, quarrels in the family are not a strange thing. Usually they are easily resolved but sometimes the problems just get worse and the longer they are left the more difficult it is to make up, creating tension and stress for everyone. All families are unique and have unique problems. There are many experienced family counsellors who have the expertise to work with you and your family to achieve the best outcome possible. Often these counsellors are found in facilities or churches or some other organisation devoted to family therapy.

13.2. Family Therapy

Family therapy, also referred to as couple and family therapy and family systems therapy, is a branch of psychotherapy related to relationship counselling that works with families and couples in intimate relationships to nurture change and development. It tends to view these in terms of the systems of interaction between family members. It emphasises family relationships as an important factor in psychological health. As such, family problems have been seen to arise as an emergent property of systemic interactions, rather than to be blamed on individual members. Marriage and Family Therapists (MFTs) are the most specifically trained in this type of psychotherapy.

Father and mother are the first role models for the children. If the character of parents is not good, it will reflect in their children also. Some parents have the habit of degrading their children according to their ability of physical appearance. Such children may later develop some mental disorders. Many of the clinical disorders of infancy, childhood, and adolescence, such as the learning disorders, communication disorders, attention-deficit and disruptive behaviour disorders, conduct disorders, and elimination disorders, as well as the general sleep disorders can all have origins within the overall family system.

Parental conflicts and family anxiety also create problems in the life of children. The increasing number of juvenile criminals tells the tales of destructive families. Personal unrest also reflects in the family and it also in a certain level affect the smooth running of a family.

Family therapists may focus more on how patterns of interaction maintain the problem rather than trying to identify the cause, as this can be experienced as blaming by some families. It assumes that the family as a whole is larger than the sum of its parts. Family therapy may also be used to draw upon the strengths of a social network to help address a problem that may be completely externally caused rather than created or maintained by the family.

13.2.1. Counselling Methods in Family Therapy

The family therapists use a range of counselling and other techniques for treating family problems. They are:

i) Communication theory
ii) Psychoeducation
iii) Psychotherapy
iv) Systemic coaching
v) Systems theory

The basic theory of classical systemic family therapy was derived mainly from systems theory and cybernetics, and secondarily from behavioural therapy and cognitive psychotherapy, although most of the founders of the field had psychoanalytic backgrounds. More recent developments have come from feminist, postmodernist, narrative, psychodynamic and attachment theories.

Once the relationship among the family members shows the sign of sores, there are a lot of ways to improve it. The important schools of family therapy include structural family therapy, strategic family therapy, a range of cognitive and behavioural approaches, constructivist, solution-focused therapy, psychodynamic, object relations, intergenerational, EFT, and experiential therapy. Multicultural, intercultural, and integrative approaches are being developed. Most practitioners claim to be "eclectic," using techniques from several areas, depending upon their own inclinations and/or the needs of the client(s).

The clients of a family therapist are not a single person. They need to meet several members of the family at the same time. This has the advantage of making differences between the ways family members perceive mutual relations as well as interaction patterns in the session apparent both for the therapist and the family. These patterns frequently mirror habitual interaction patterns at home, even though the therapist is now incorporated into the family system.

The therapist analyse the relationship between the family members rather than on analysing impulses of the unconscious mind or early childhood trauma of individuals. Although some schools of family therapy do consider such individual and historical factors, and they may use instruments such as the genogram to help to elucidate the patterns of relationship across generations.

For giving adequate guidance to the clients, a family therapist must be a rational thinker. Family therapy is really a way of thinking, an epistemology rather than about how many people sit in the room with the therapist. Family therapists are relational therapists; they are generally more interested in what goes between people rather than in people.

Depending on circumstances, a therapist may point out to the family interaction patterns that the family might have not noticed; or suggest different ways of responding to other family members. These changes in the way of responding may then trigger repercussions in the whole system, leading to a more satisfactory systemic state.

13.2.2 Principles in Family Therapy

Today, marital problems are very common in the society. The society is giving lots of freedom to the couples and the misuse of such freedom always creates problems. While handling clients from a family, the therapists insist on keeping values and ethics very effectively. For the sake of family, the therapist keeps some matters without disclosing to anybody.

Family therapy aims to improve troubled relationships. The common issues in a family are:

— Marital problems
— Divorce
— Eating disorders, such as anorexia or bulimia
— Substance abuse
— Depression or bipolar disorder
— Chronic health problems, such as asthma or cancer
— Grief, loss and trauma
— Work stress
— Parenting skills
— Emotional abuse or violence
— Financial problems

If a member in the family has a mental problem, mental health treatment should also be done along with family therapy. Family therapy isn't a substitute for other necessary treatments. For instance, family therapy can help family members cope if a relative has schizophrenia. But the person with schizophrenia should continue with his or her individualised treatment plan, such as medication and possibly hospitalisation.

Sometimes, the persons in trouble get legal protection. Adolescents in trouble with the law may be ordered into family therapy rather than serving jail time, for instance. Violent or abusive parents are sometimes spared jail if they enter family therapy. Divorcing couples may also be required to attend family therapy.

13.2.3. Conducting Family Therapy

Normally, the therapy is conducting for the entire family members. However, family members may also see a family therapist individually. Family therapy can even include non-family members, such as teachers, other health care providers or representatives of social services agencies.

When the problems in a family express in front of full family members, it is easy to solve it. You may explore family roles, rules and behaviour patterns in order to spot issues that contribute to conflict. Family therapy may help you identify your family's strengths, such as caring for one another, and weaknesses, such as an inability to confide in one other.

13.2.4. Assistance for Reuniting Couples

Marriage is a very sacred relation. It is the union of two individuals who are coming from different provenance. It's based in a commitment to protecting family and children, and grounded in the concept of a man and a woman giving themselves to each other for life in order to bring new life into the world: to have children and to create a family in which the children are raised to honour such values as faith, hope, and charity-not to fear love. The conjugal act between the man and the woman guarantees this generation of life. Marriage, therefore, is an act of service, not a psychological way to soothe your fear of emptiness through a "relationship" with another person.

Marriage also brings love, affection, togetherness, commitments, etc. All the moral decisions about marriage and family actually derive psychologically from love-real love, not the "love" of popular fantasy. Infidelity, contraception, abortion, divorce, euthanasia, and even embryonic stem-cell research, all defile love through a focus on personal pleasure and convenience, at the expense of the dignity-and even the life-of another human being.

But today, love is a way to find personal fulfilment in life. That is, each person in a "relationship" expects the other to fill up the existential void in his or her life. Ultimately, this is impossible, and so when there are problems, the conflicts are usually about one person complaining of not getting what he or she wants. In this situation, only one psychological solution can be possible: Take responsibility for your own life satisfaction. True love is about giving, not receiving. If you're mainly concerned about getting pleasure or security, you're being selfish, not loving.

For getting love and emotional security, one should stop blaming others. If you are not satisfied with your life, it's probably because you are not living up to your inner potential or are in one way or another betraying your life values. Skirmishes in marriages are inevitable. But when these fights lead to big conflicts, the couples need counselling and therapy. Marriage counselling gives couples the tools to communicate better, negotiate differences, problem solve and even argue in a healthier way.

13.3. Couples Therapy

Marriage is the union of two independent individuals. So, in couple's counselling, therapist handles the problem of individuals and the couple's relationship. Typically, both partners in the relationship attend the counselling session to discuss the couple's specific issues. The aim of couple's counselling is to help a couple deals appropriately with their immediate problems and to learn better ways of relating in general.

Couples therapy or couple's counselling is a useful modality of help for couples who are experiencing difficulties such as repetitive arguments, feelings of distance or emptiness in the relationship, pervasive feelings of anger, resentment and or dissatisfaction or lack of interest in affection or in a physical relationship with one another.

Today, the feeling of isolation among the couples is increasing and the couples are expected to manage their lives and families without the community supports that in the past were a primary resource in raising children and meeting family needs. Couples in our present culture are less bound by family traditions and are freer than ever before to develop relationships unlike those of the families that they were raised in. With the aid of a qualified clinician, couples can bring peace, stability and communication back into their relationship thus affecting their lives and the lives of those most impacted by them and their relationship.

13.4. Imago Relationship Therapy

Family therapy aims to solve problems among the couples and family. Some couples may doubtful about the efficiency of the counselling. While some may choose to terminate the relationship, we would much prefer a couple to stay together. With a whopping national divorce rate, new methods of approaching marital conflict are necessary.

Nowadays, Imago Relationship Therapy is getting popular its effectiveness in healing the ruptures in relationships and making room for passion. One of the best things about Imago is its emphasis on safety. Therapy is no longer to confirm what you already know is wrong about your spouse or to convince the therapist to align with you, but a realisation that whatever is going on in the relationship is equally due to both of you. The only way to redevelop trust and rekindle connection is to feel safe. If you do not feel safe you cannot fully show up with your entire being in a relationship.

We all do not like to hear that we are responsible for the discord. Any one us encourage to be blamed in front of others. This model only contributes to further discord. Creating an atmosphere of safety makes seeking assistance much more inviting. Safety must be primary in any counselling experience, as without it one cannot rekindle connection.

If the therapy is very structured, it ensures safety. The therapist acts as facilitator, making sure couples follow the process and remain in connection. They face each other, looking towards each other, not the therapist, to heal the rupture in their relationship. More important than solving a particular problem is the maintenance of connection, for once one problem is solved, another will arise. The best gift we can give to couples is tools which assist them in developing the sacred space of their relationship, so that they are able to tackle any issue that confronts them and emerge intact. As couples become dialogical, their whole way of being is safe and invites relationship.

The structure of Imago is what allows the passion to re-emerge in our interpersonal relationships. The discipline of dialogue brings about centering and connection. When both parties feel safe, the walls between them that did such a great job of protecting them are no longer necessary. A wall is only needed when there is perceived danger. In addition, there is no longer a need to pry or to force insight, for when we feel safe, insight will come out. Couples are now able to share, to listen, and to heal, making the journey from conflict to compassion. When we place safety first, we contain the fire of volatility that too often plagues marriages and rekindle the flame of passion.

13.5. Counselling for a Long Lasting Marital Relationship

Marriages are meant for long lasting togetherness. But conflicts make marital life a hell. Couselling helps infighting couples to build a healthy and long lasting relationship. It can be a worthwhile investment for the long-term, providing couples with the skills and strategies they need to manage life together in a healthy way. With increasing divorce rates and millions of couples who are simply unsatisfied with their relationship, an intervention from a professional counsellor can be the necessary step for improving the relationship, helping everyone work on key issues that are causing conflict, and working towards improvement with each session.

Marriage counselling is not just for unhappy couples; it can be a valuable addition to any relationship since it gives each person involved fundamental tools and healthy coping strategies to manage their communication, show respect for each other, and grow in healthy ways.

13.5.1. Healing through Marriage Counselling

Ideological differences are common in every marital life. But when it becomes serious, couples need the help of counsellors to get out of the problem. Most people are simply not equipped with healthy communication skills and managing distress in a productive way; this itself is often the cause of many interpersonal and marital problems. However, these can all be learned with experience and guidance. Marriage counselling can help a couple resolve a crisis, improve communications, and even help with healing after a difficult period or time of transition. Marriage counselling removes sulkiness and negative behaviour from a relationship, or help couples work on healthy life and coping skills so that they can manage stress, conflict, and any other problems in their relationship in a positive way.

The couples in infighting may not ready to forgive and forget. Instead, they may wait for another chance to fight against the partner. Negotiating differences and resolving problems are also challenges in marital relation. Marriage counselling helps by giving couples the tools they need to gain perspective and work on ways to establish healthy boundaries during conflict. Instead of stepping into crisis mode each time a difficulty arises, marriage counselling works to prevent negative behaviour and attitudes, focusing instead on a results-oriented approach that can benefit both parties.

Unemployment, job transitions, or career changes can also put stress on a couple. Learning how to be empathetic, managing finances effectively during difficult times, and difficult life events, can put a lot of pressure on a couple and make a negative situation worse very quickly. Marriage counselling helps couples cope with challenges and stressors by providing resources and healthy strategies of managing the situation. As a result, couples can look forward to an improved outlook and communicate with one another in a healthy way.

Marriage counselling sometimes works with couples in a joint therapy setting; this helps couples communicate their feelings, thoughts, and perspective about a situation in a neutral setting with a therapist nearby for guidance and support. Counsellors and therapists can help each individual learn to share their feelings with honesty and communicate these ideas effectively to the other person. Open communication with the therapist can be critical for growth, and marriage counselling helps couples take part in regular sessions to determine and address the root cause of the problem.

13.5.2. Beneficiaries of Family Counselling

In this selfish world, not only marriages but all relationships are degrading. We are not ready to accept the abilities of others. Instead of seeking good qualities, all are interested in the bad qualities of others. Each person brings his or her own ideas, values, opinions and personal history into a relationship, and they don't always match their partner's. Those differences don't necessarily mean your relationship is bound for conflict. To the contrary, differences can be complementary—you know the saying about opposites attracting. These differences can also help people understand, respect and accept opposing views and cultures.

It doesn't mean that we should believe everybody. If we believe each one blindly, that will be the starting point of our failure. Relationships can be tested. Differences or habits that you once found endearing may grate on your nerves after time together. Sometimes specific issues, such as an extramarital affair or loss of sexual attraction, trigger problems in a relationship. Other times, there's a gradual disintegration of communication and caring.

Whatever may be the reason, distress in a relationship can create undue stress, tension, sadness, worry, fear and other problems. You may hope your relationship troubles just go away on their own. But left to fester, a bad relationship may only worsen and eventually lead to physical or psychological problems, such as depression. A bad relationship can also create problems on the job and affect other family members or even friendships as people feel compelled to take sides.

The common issues crop up in marriages are:

- Infidelity
- Divorce
- Substance abuse
- Physical or mental conditions
- Same-sex relationship issues
- Cultural clashes
- Finances
- Unemployment
- Blended families
- Communication problems
- Sexual difficulties
- Conflicts about child rearing
- Infertility
- Anger
- Changing roles, such as retirement

Counselling helps to sort out all these problems. It is also helpful for domestic violence or abuse. However, if the abuse or violence has escalated to the point that you fear for your safety or that of your children, consider contacting the police or a local shelter or crisis center. Relaying on marriage counselling alone will not help to resolve these problems.

Marriage counselling is not meant for only reuniting a troubled relationship. It also helps to strengthen the bonds and gain a better understanding of each other. Marriage counselling can also help couples who plan to get married. This pre-marriage counselling can help you achieve a deeper understanding of each other and iron out differences before a union is sealed.

13.6. Factors for Successful Counselling

13.6.1. Motivation

We all have our own concept on life. Dialogical differences and different viewpoints on life also create problems. Unless we ready to change from our way of thinking, clonselling may not give any change in life. They want others to change; they want their environment or circumstances to change but they are resistant to doing anything different themselves.

Change is not a simple task. It is painful because they have difficulty embracing the idea of change. Many individuals have difficulty with the process of change because it can create much anxiety getting outside one's comfort zone. For some, it's just being a creature of habit and the known is more preferable than the unknown. New habits, new methods of doing things, and changing thinking patterns or behaviours take a great deal of energy and time, as well as courage.

Change demands courage. Given the choice of being with someone who is courageous or someone who is fearless, choose the courageous person. Anyone who is without fear can be a danger to you because they will take risks that could get you hurt. The person with courage is willing to do what it takes and will most likely be more careful about it because they do experience fear. They are not paralysed by fear; they are empowered by it. Seeking help and making changes in your life requires courage. If you are willing to be different you are about a quarter of the way to having a better life.

13.6.2. Inspiration

Inspiration or motivation is an essential quality for making a change in the life. If a person doesn't have the adequate motivation, he simply undergoes therapy and they will express a desire for change but will not make the effort necessary to actually carry out the process.

People seek counselling when their life may have deteriorated to the point of being in a state of crisis. They may have become entangled in the legal system; been threatened with loss of their marriage or family; or in danger of losing their jobs. In addition, they may also be in emotional pain over such a length time that their health has become an issue.

A crisis can be a life disaster or calamity but it can also be a means to making life better because it provides a motivation for personal growth and development. Without a strong drive for change, it is less likely to happen. When an individual has both the willingness to improve and the motivation to do so, they have half of what it takes to succeed in the counselling process.

13.6.3. Dedication

People tend to be impatient with the personal growth process. Most of us are impatient or lack the maturity to suffer delayed gratification will express this urgency along with those who are experiencing enormous distress in their life. Those who have patients are ready for a change and they make benefit out of counselling.

Without commitment and patience, many will rush into what they think is a viable solution but eventually find the problem has not really been resolved at all.

13.6.4. Faith

The lack of faith is the root cause for most of the problems in a marital life. If the couples are not faithful, it is impossible to accomplish any project or task. In other words, the more you believe in something, the more you increase your chances of being successful at it.

Fidelity has very important role in marriage. The concept of belief in oneself or belief in a process seems simple and we can usually agree about the necessity of it, but there are still those who fail because they do not possess the strength of faith to accomplish their goals.

If a person do not believe in counselling or a counsellor, undergoing family therapy will become meaningless. They have seen multimedia programmes that disparage individuals who seek counselling, or portray counsellors and psychotherapists in an unflattering manner. Some may view counselling as for the weak and cowardly. Each person fails when they have little or no faith in the healing process of change.

The successful individual understands that it takes believing in yourself and in others to accomplish a goal or task. They realise that a certain amount of trust needs to be placed in a well-trained, well-educated health care provider or at least explore their lack of trust issues with the therapist in the beginning phase of counselling.

The lack of trust in others may stem from early childhood issues and be a primary source of a person's pain. Overcoming adversity and gaining achievement is a culmination of all four attributes of willingness, motivation, commitment, and faith, and with them you can have a complete opportunity of success in therapy as well as any reasonable goals you set in life.

13.7. Conclusion

Family is the cradle for comfort and affection. Marriage life is the confluence of two different personalities coming from difference provenance. Husband and wife is the sole determinant for making their life a heaven or hell. If the parents are good, the children also follow their path and acquire good qualities from them. All of us mould our character from the family. If marriage works, it is the most beautiful place to live in. But when it becomes conflicts, family needs counselling then. Here lies the importance of family counselling.

References

Lebow, J., "Guidelines for Conducting Couple and Family Therapy", In G. Koocker, J.C. Norcross, & S.S. Hill (eds.), *Psychologists Desk Reference (2 nd edition.),* New York: Oxford Press, 2004

_______________ ., "Family Therapy in the 21 st Century", In Lebow, J.(ed.) *Handbook of Clinical Family Therapy,* John Wiley & Sons, 2004.

Pinsof, W., "A Shamanic Tapesty: My Experiences with Individual, Marital, and Family Therapy", In Geller, J.D., Norcross, J.C. and Orlinsky, D.E. (Eds.), *The Psychotherapist's Own Psychotherapy: Patient and Clinician Perspectives,* New York: Oxford University Press, 2004

Wolff, M.; Krefman, K. and Martin, P., "Maintaining or Enhancing Couple and Family Relationships in the Face of Dementia", *Buehler Center on Aging Magazine,* Summer, 2004.

14

Expressive Therapy

14.1. Introduction

Healthy mind is a blessing. We all like to keep our mind hilarious always. But unfortunately, in this tensed world, it is very difficult keep a healthy mind. However, we can attain mental health in a certain level by engaging in some interested activities such plays. Expressive therapy, also known as creative arts therapy, is the intentional use of the creative arts as a form of process art therapy. Unlike traditional art expression, the process of creation is emphasised rather than the final aesthetic product. Expressive therapy works under the assumption that through use of imagination and the various forms of creative expression, humans can heal.

The activities which reveal tensions are dance, music, drama, culture, art, etc. Expressive therapists are often known as dance therapists, art therapists, music therapists, drama therapists and as other names based on their choice of primary artistic expression, also known as their modality. All expressive therapists share the belief that it is through creative expression and the tapping of the imagination a person can examine the body, feelings, emotions and his or her thought process.

Expressive therapists work with a wide variety of populations in a wide variety of environments. They have worked in areas such as medical illness, grief, educational and behavioral problems, emotional issues, and even criminal behaviour.

14.2. Art Therapy

All of us have certain abilities and personal choices. The busy life style may prevent us to fulfill such abilities. The art therapy, a form of expressive therapy, helps us to take out our qualities such as paints, chalk and markers. Art therapy combines traditional psychotherapeutic theories and techniques with an understanding of the psychological aspects of the creative process, especially the affective properties of the different art materials.

Art therapy is employed in many clinical settings with diverse populations. Art therapy can be found in non-clinical settings as well, such as in art studios and in workshops that focus on creativity development. Art therapists work with children, adolescents, and adults and provide services to individuals, couples, families, groups, and communities.

Art therapy is based on the belief that the creative process of art is both healing and life-enhancing. Art therapists use the creative process and the issues that come up during art therapy to help their clients increase insight and judgment, cope better with stress, work through traumatic experiences, increase cognitive abilities, have better relationships with family and friends, and to just be able to enjoy the life-affirming pleasures of the creative experience. The term art therapist is reserved for those that are professionals trained in both art and therapy and hold a master's degree in art therapy or a related field.

14.2.1 Objectives of Art Therapy

For improving mental health, art therapy has an important role. But whereas some of the other expressive therapies utilise the performing arts for expressive purposes, art therapy generally utilises drawing, painting, sculpture, photography, and other forms of visual art expression.

Art therapists are trained to recognise the nonverbal symbols and metaphors that are communicated within the creative process, symbols and metaphors which might be difficult to express in words or in other modalities. By helping their clients to discover what underlying thoughts and feelings are being communicated in the artwork and what it means to them, it is hoped that clients will not only gain insight and judgment, but perhaps develop a better understanding of themselves and the way they relate to the people around them.

Art therapy is conducted by trained therapists. There are many psychological assessments that utilise artmaking to analyse various types of mental functioning. Many art therapists eschew diagnostic testing and indeed some writers question the validity of therapists making interpretative assumptions. A few most common art therapy assessments are:

14.2.1.1. Diagnostic Drawing Series (DDS)

This method is used for assessing a range of major psychiatric disorders. There are three parts to the DDS. In the first part, the patient is asked to draw any picture using coloured chalk pastels and then they are asked to draw a tree in the second part. In the last part of the test, the patient is asked to show how they are feeling using lines, shapes, and colours. The series of pictures are interpreted based on a combination of many different factors, such as use of colour, amount of blending, and placement of the images on the paper.

14.2.1.2. Mandala Assessment Research Instrument (MARI)

Here, a person is asked to select a card from a deck with different mandalas; designs enclosed in a geometric shape, and then must choose a color from a set of coloured cards. The person is then asked to draw the mandala from the card they choose with an oil pastel of the colour of their choice. The artist is then asked to explain if there were any meanings, experiences, or related information related to the mandala they drew. This test assesses and gives clues to a person's psychological progressions and their current psychological condition. The mandala originates in Buddhism.

14.2.1.3. House-Tree-Person (HTP)

Here, patient has to draw a picture with a house, a tree, and a person in it. This is a projective assessment and the house, the tree, and person in the drawing represent different aspects of the artist and the way the artist feels about him or herself.

14.3. Dance Therapy

This therapy uses dance movements for treating depression. It is the psychotherapeutic use of movement (and dance) for emotional, cognitive, social, behavioural and physical conditions.

It is a form of expressive therapy. Certified dance therapists hold a masters level of training.

The body and mind are an interrelated continuum, that the state of the body may affect mental and emotional wellbeing in manifold ways. In contrast to artistic dance, which is usually concerned with the aesthetic appearance of movement, dance therapy explores the nature of all movement. Through observing and altering the kinesthetic movements of a client, dance movement therapists diagnose and help solve various psychological problems. As any conscious person can move on some level, this therapy can work with any population.

14.4. Drama Therapy

While involving in drama, we forget our tensions and enjoy the art. This is the principle of drama therapy. Drama therapy is an expressive therapy modality used in a wide variety of settings, including hospitals, schools, mental health centers, prisons, and businesses. Drama therapy exists in many forms and can be applicable to individuals, couples, families, and various groups.

The use of dramatic process and theater as a therapeutic intervention began with Psychodrama. The field has expanded to allow many forms of theatrical interventions as therapy including role-play, theater games, group-dynamic games, mime, puppetry, and other improvisational techniques. Often, drama therapy is utilised to help a client:

— Solve a problem
— Achieve a catharsis
— Delve into truths about self
— Understand the meaning of personally resonate images
— Explore and transcend unhealthy patterns of interaction

Based on the practitioner, drama therapy is extremely varied in its use. From fully-fledged performances to empty chair role-play, the sessions may involve many variables including the use of a troupe of actors.

14.5. Music Therapy

Music has a magical power to alleviagte all our tensions. Music therapy is the clinical and evidence-based use of music interventions to accomplish individualised goals within a therapeutic relationship by a qualified professional who has completed an approved music therapy programme.

Music therapy is the use of music by a trained professional to achieve therapeutic goals. Goal areas include, but are not limited to, motor skills, social/interpersonal development, cognitive development, self-awareness, and spiritual enhancement. Music therapy is now an established health service similar to occupational therapy and physical therapy. Music therapists use music to facilitate changes that are non-musical in nature. The use of music for those with arthritis provides opportunity for pain relief, anxiety and stress reduction and positive changes in both mood and emotional state.

Music is a widely used therapy. Such therapists are also found in nearly every area of the helping professions. Some commonly found practices include developmental work with individuals with special needs, songwriting and listening in reminiscence/orientation work with the elderly, processing and relaxation work, and rhythmic entrainment for physical rehabilitation in stroke victims.

14.6. Play Therapy

Generally, this therapy is used for children with mental disorders. Play provides a way for children to express their experiences and feelings through a natural, self-guided, self-healing process. As children's experiences and knowledges are often communicated through play, it becomes an important vehicle for them to know and accept themselves and others.

This Therapy is the systematic use of a theoretical model to establish an interpersonal process wherein play therapists use the therapeutic powers of play to help clients prevent or resolve psychosocial challenges and achieve optimal growth and development. A working definition might be a form of counseling or psychotherapy that therapeutically engages the power of play to communicate with and help people, especially children, to engender optimal integration and individuation.

Play Therapy is often used as tool of diagnosis. A play therapist observes a client playing with toys (play-houses, pets, dolls, etc) to determine the cause of the disturbed behaviour. The objects and patterns of play, as well as the willingness to interact with the therapist can be used to understand the underlying rationale for behavior both inside and outside the session.

People will engage in play behaviour in order to work through their interior obfuscations and anxieties. In this way play therapy can be used as a self-help mechanism, as long as children are allowed time for "free play" or "unstructured play." From a developmental point of view, play has been determined to be an essential component of healthy child development. Play has been directly linked to cognitive development.

Play therapists use a type of systematic desensitisation or relearning therapy to change the disturbing behaviour, either systematically or in less formal social settings. These processes are normally used with children, but are also applied with other pre-verbal, non-verbal, or verbally-impaired persons, such as slow-learners, brain-injured or drug-affected persons. Mature adults usually need much "group permission" before indulging in the relaxed spontaneity of play therapy, so a very skilled group worker is needed to deal with such guarded individuals.

14.6.1. Effectiveness of Play Therapy

Play therapy is very much useful for treating children with aggressiveness. An extensive body of literature has documented the effectiveness of play therapy, as a counselling model, in working with children and adolescents. The effectiveness of play therapy related to conduct disorder, aggression and oppositional behavior have been undertaken.

Play therapy at first helps to build a relationship with a child and the therapist. This relationship is a very important tool in the therapeutic process because a child or adolescent will more readily talk about their intimate feelings when they feel respected and accepted.

There after, the therapist uses specific techniques to assess how a child or adolescent experience their world and how they communicate and react to the events and people in their world. Children are lead to become aware of what they are feeling and opportunities are given to express these feelings. Awareness is a very important process in play therapy, because without awareness change is not possible.

Throughout the therapy the child or adolescent is empowered and supported to learn more about who they are, to talk about things that are frightening or painful, to be self supportive and to experiment with new behaviour.

14.6.2. Benefits of Play Therapy

Children over the age of four years are the great beneficiaries of play therapy. It can help to become aware of what feelings and how these feelings manifest in behaviour or one's body. They can learn how to become better at regulating emotions and expressing them in constructive ways. They can discover who they are and what their strong and weak points, needs, wishes, thoughts and dreams are. The combination of this self-knowledge and training in social skills may help a child to become more assertive, self-confident and to have self-respect and respect for others.

14.6.3. Principles of Play Therapy

In childhood, humans use less language because the development of language lags behind the cognitive development. So, children communicate their awareness of what is happening in their world through their play. In play therapy toys are viewed as the child's words and play as the child's language-a language of activity. Play therapy, then, is to children what counseling or psychotherapy is to adults. In play therapy the symbolic function of play is what is so important, providing children with a means of expressing their inner world. Emotionally significant experiences can be expressed more comfortably and safely through the symbolic representation the toys provide.

The use of toys enables children to transfer anxieties, fears, fantasies, and guilt to objects rather than people. In the process, children are safe from their own feelings and reactions because play enables children to distance themselves from traumatic events and experiences. Therefore, children are not overwhelmed by their own actions because the act takes place in fantasy. By acting out through play a frightening or traumatic experience or situation symbolically, and perhaps changing or reversing the outcome in the play activity, children move toward an inner resolution, and then they are better able to cope with or adjust to problems.

The play process also allows children to consider new possibilities not possible in reality, thus greatly expanding the expression of self. In the safety of the play therapy experience, children explore the unfamiliar and develop a knowing that is both experiential-feeling and cognitive. It can then be said that through the process of play therapy, the unfamiliar becomes familiar, and children express outwardly through play what has taken place inwardly. A major function of play in play therapy is the changing of what may be unmanageable in reality to manageable situations through symbolic representation, which provides children opportunities for learning to cope.

14.6.4. Method of Play Therapy

Children express their feelings and emotions through play. Although the dynamics of expression and the vehicle for communication are different for children, the expressions (fear, satisfaction, anger, happiness, frustration, contentment) are similar to those of adults. Children may have considerable difficulty trying to tell what they feel or how their experiences have affected them. If permitted, however, in the presence of a caring, sensitive, and empathetic adult, they will reveal inner feelings through the toys and materials they choose what they do with and to the materials, and the stories they act out.

The child creates his/her own world through play. By using play therapy, the therapist make a relation between the child and allow his/her to explore more in his/her own world. Play therapy provides an opportunity for children to live out, during play, experiences and associated feelings. This process allows the therapist to experience, in a personal and interactive way, the inner dimensions of the child's world. This therapeutic relationship is what provides dynamic growth and healing for the child.

The world of children is a world of action and activity. Play therapy provides the therapist with an opportunity to enter the child's world. The child is not restricted to discussing what happened; rather, the child lives out at the moment of play the past experience and associated feelings. If the reason the child was referred to the therapist is aggressive behaviour, the medium of play gives the therapist an opportunity to experience the aggression firsthand as the child bangs on the Bobo or attempts to shoot the therapist with a gun and also to help the child learn self-control by responding with appropriate therapeutic limit-setting procedures.

Without the presence of play materials, the therapist could only talk with the child about the aggressive behavior the child exhibited yesterday or last week. In play therapy, whatever the reason for referral, the therapist has the opportunity to experience and actively deal with that problem in the immediacy of the child's experiencing. Axline viewed this process as one in which the child plays out feelings, bringing them to the surface, getting them out in the open, facing them, and either learning to control them or abandon them.

14.6.5. Future of Play Therapy

The field of play therapy is growing rapidly. Increasing numbers of elementary school counsellors and therapists in private practice and agencies are incorporating play therapy into their work with children. There is a trend in family therapy to address social and emotional values of developmental as well as family group session issues. In filial therapy, parents are trained to use play therapy procedures with their children. This method is well researched and has proven to be effective in ameliorating children's problems through enhancing the parent-child relationship.

14.7. Conclusion

An uncontrollable expression of our feelings, emotions and abilities are the foundation stone of expressive therapy. While our mind is indulge in interesting activities, we get less time for the things which pestering us. This is the basic principle of this therapy. More over, by indulging in the activities we like, we liberate our mind from the control of tensions and sorrows. Then, we are ready to think calmly to find out the real reason behind our mental torture.

References

Axline, V.M., *Play therapy: The inner dynamics of childhood*, Cambridge, MA: Houghton Mifflin, 1947.

Landreth, G.L., *Play therapy: The art of the relationship*, Munice, IN: Accelerated Development, 1991.

________________., Homeyer, L., Glover, G., & Sweeney, D., *Play therapy interventions with children's problems*, Northvale, NJ: Jason Aronson, 1996.

15

Exposure Therapy

15.1. Introduction

People may come across with mental disorders due to certain phobias such as a feared situation, object, thought, or memory. The fear deposits in their inner minds and whenever they meet with such situations, tremble with fear uncontrollably.

Exposure therapy deals with patients having such phobias. Sometimes, exposure therapy involves reliving a traumatic experience in a controlled, therapeutic environment. The goal of exposure therapy is to reduce the distress, physical or emotional, felt in certain situations. Exposure therapy may be used in dealing with anxiety, phobias, and post-traumatic stress.

The therapist who is practising exposure therapy helps the patient remember a disturbing thought, traumatic situation, or feared object. The therapist also helps the patient deal with the unpleasant emotions or physical symptoms that may arise from this exposure. Through confronting the situations and thoughts that cause stress, patients are often able to learn coping skills, eventually reducing or even eliminating symptoms.

An open discussion helps to sort out problems in the sub conscious mind of the patients. The first step of the therapist is to make a rapport with the patient. Such friendships empower the patient to disclose his inner feelings to the therapist. The patients are also encouraged to learn new ways of viewing fears and distressing situations. Hypnosis is sometimes used as part of this type of therapy. Even virtual reality techniques are used at times.

Techniques of relaxation are taught as part of exposure therapy. These techniques may be very helpful in dealing with both physical and emotional distress. They are intended to help the patient maintain control, even when faced with the situation, object, or thought that causes fear or distress. Often, breathing exercises can be effective interventions taught in conjunction with exposure therapy.

Exposure therapy is sometimes compared to desensitisation. Unlike desensitisation, however, exposure therapy produces anxiety in the patient on purpose. Desensitisation, on the other hand, combines relaxation with gradual introduction to the anxiety-producing object, thought, or situation. Furthermore, exposure therapy involves exposing the patient to the most distressing thought or situation first, while systematic desensitisation begins with that which causes the least fear.

Flooding or graduated techniques are also included in exposure therapy. When flooding techniques are used, the patient may be exposed to the frightening or distressing thought, situation, or object for as much as two hours at a time. Graduated techniques are considered gentler because the patient may face the distressing stimuli in shorter chunks of time and have more control over the duration of the exposure.

15.2. Intensive Exposure Therapy

Intensive exposure therapy is used to treat people with specific phobias, such as fear of flying. It is a process in which the phobic person is exposed to the feared situations or objects. The therapy may be done "in vivo" (the person is actually exposed to the real situations or objects) or through visualisation techniques.

Exposure therapy may be done quickly or slowly. Systematic desensitisation is the gradual exposure to feared situations or objects. Intensive exposure therapy, also called "flooding," is the rapid exposure to feared situations. Through exposure, the phobic person comes to see that the situation or object will not cause harm.

With systematic desensitisation, the phobic person stays in the situation until the panic levels are no longer manageable. Coping techniques, such as breathing exercises, are used to make the manageable period longer each time of exposure. With intensive exposure therapy, usually the phobic person stays and experiences intense panic, learning that these feelings will not cause harm.

Exposure therapy is often part of cognitive-behavioural treatment programmes for phobias, including agoraphobia. What is controversial is whether or not the therapy should be a quick or slow process. The effectiveness of intensive exposure therapy would depend on the individual. The center for anxiety and related disorders has apparently had success in using intensive exposure therapy in treating panic disorder.

A combination of medication and cognitive-behavioural is the most effective treatment for most individuals with panic disorder. Panic disorder is a complex condition, often made more complex with the co-existence of other conditions, mainly depression and/ or other anxiety disorders.

15.2.1. Treating Social Anxiety Disorder

Anxiety creates phobias in a certain extend. Exposure therapy is suggested to be one of the best ways to overcome anxiety. For implementing it in a very effective way, one should actually need to go into the situation and think about it in a different way, implement the other skills and knowledge you have to mange your anxiety, and then reflect on how it went.

The mentality of the people is different from person to person. Some people can alleviate fear by facing it. For some, it doesn't. Learning the skills and techniques of cognitive therapy and educating yourself on where your anxiety is actually coming from in the first place, prior to exposing yourself to the situation, can often have better outcomes as you can feel more in control before you enter the situation, rather than going in feeling absolutely terrified.

To ward off anxiety, one should allow passing the fear through their mind and then facing the situation of fear. This is called exposure therapy. Avoidance of fearful situation only hardens to overcome anxiety. When you avoid doing something, you often convince yourself that there is a very good reason why you are not doing it. If you continue to avoid situations, no amount of thinking about it in another way will actually help you overcome your anxiety in the situations. The more often you do something, the easier it becomes each time.

15.2.2. Exposure Therapy for PTSD

Exposure therapy is a deliberate method designed to expose the mind to intense emotional fear in controlled doses, and teach your body that it now not need be disturbed by traumatic memories, as they are just memories, and that you do not any longer have to take seriously these unbidden memories of your past traumatic experience. Exposure therapy is a learning strategy simply designed to separate 'then' from 'now.'

Exposure therapy does not make up the entirety of Cognitive Behavioural Therapy (CBT), as many facets are required to complete the overall healing process, though exposure therapy is certainly a good portion of the trauma healing process.

15.2.3. Criteria for Choosing Exposure Therapy

The consumption of alcohol or drugs adversely affect exposure therapy. So, the patient should be free from the use of all such things. Otherwise it gives only negative results.

The objective behind the selection of exposure therapy is that you need to come to terms with the full reality of your trauma, and no longer continue that you have it under control with your current coping strategies, which are more often than not, non effective. While many think they have their symptoms under control with alcohol usage, smoking a joint per day, dedicating yourself to working long hours or maintaining a busy lifestyle, each and every time, you end up back at the beginning, with your symptoms prevailing over you, and not you over them.

These types of strategies are not actually coping mechanisms at all, and merely delusional suppressants which are proven non-effective. If you're still having nightmares, still having flashbacks, and still suffering symptoms arising daily / weekly from PTSD, then your strategies are not working for you. You must push yourself from this point past your comfort zone, into an area you have avoided for so long, though an area which must be dealt with to move past the worst of PTSD itself.

When you forcibly forget some memories, it comes back to you with multiple energies. Ineffective methods which only tighten the elastic band, and make it pull back more each time you push it away from you. Exposure therapy turns these painful, hurtful memories that you fear, into what they actually are, just memories of the bad times within your past. You will no longer ignore them, but accept them and come to terms with them being part of your past, but without the fear and pain associated to them.

15.2.4. Effective Strategies

Effective strategies for exposure therapy are:

- — Writing about the trauma for at a set time for a couple of minutes.
- — Typing something for a few minutes a day (the lesser stressful option).
- — Talking with a confidant for a few minutes each day.
- — Spending a few minutes daily talking and listening to a audio recording of yourself (not recommended for trauma from horror).
- — Setting dares to extend you beyond your comfort levels.
- — Writing about the trauma and its effects in a more documentary style.

These strategies help a person to combat with fearful memories.

15.2.4. Consequences

While undergoing exposure therapy, expect to have an increase in negative mood, an increase in symptoms, and a definite impact from your increased mood on friends, family and partners, all of whom may discourage you continuing exposure therapy, as it will negatively impact them also, but a little pre-warning can get around this negative feedback from your support cell. This is short term pain, for long term gain. It is effective, it is proven, and it factually lessens the effect of trauma upon the mind and body, thus having a carry on effect to all other symptoms of PTSD, as the trauma is the ignition of all other symptoms.

15.2.5. Methods for a Successful Recover

Dares is the effective method for a successful recovery. These are the therapeutic antidote to the safety behaviours involving learning not so much at an intellectual but primarily at an experiential level, in the gut. Basically, if you look at how a young child can be taught to not be afraid of the water, they gradually increase the dares as such that are performed in learning to swim at the experiential level (doing) rather than the learning of physics principles, which is what then gives them the confidence to float at a basic level.

Dares are identified between closing the gap between current behaviours, opposed to pre-trauma behaviours. If you used to be capable to going to a crowed shopping centre, or standing in long waiting lines at the checkout, and now cannot, then these would facilitate the dares that you need to perform. These range across your entire behavioural patterns, and are not just limited to one or two of your symptomatic responses now.

Experiential learning can only be accomplished by triggering the amygdala to the alarm position, which then the alarm rings and it will be quite uncomfortable to you, though afterwards the alarm will come back a notch. The payoff for the alarm coming back a notch is that you will begin to notice improved patterns, ie, sleep will improve with less need for sentry duty, concentration will improve with less effort focused upon your traumas, and the list carries on.

To prevent avoidance dares must be time-tabled. The intent of dares is not to be at ease afterwards, but instead disconfirm there expectations that you have created, and learn to tolerate rather than remove distressing emotions. Intentionally inducing the internal alarm to panic is so that the body and mind can see and learn that nothing terrible actually does happen. It is about beating your own thoughts and perceptions that you have now come to believe are reality, when in fact, they are just thoughts and perceptions, and not reality.

15.3. Extermination and Exposure Therapy

Systematic desensitisation is based on an essential misperception of the laws of classical conditioning. Classical conditioning is essentially ephemeral. Organisms stop responding to the conditioned stimulus when it is no longer paired with the unconditioned stimulus. In the process of extinction, when conditioned stimuli lose their capacity to elicit a response when they are presented too many times in the absence of the unconditioned stimulus.

Phobic reactions essentially involve two learning processes: classical conditioning, to instill the anxiety response to a previously neutral stimulus; and operant conditioning, to reinforce the voluntary escape or avoidance behaviours that remove the patient from the presence of the conditioned stimulus before the anxious arousal can be extinguished. In essence, people who acquire a phobic reaction to a basically benign stimulus don't extinguish, because they don't stay in the situation long enough for classical extinction to take place.

Although systematic desensitisation was undoubtedly effective, it was unnecessarily complex and time consuming. The essential mechanism of change, they suggested, was extinction, not counterconditioning, and the only procedure needed was to expose the patient repeatedly to the feared object or situation. Of course, the therapist would also have to do something to prevent the patient from running away or otherwise terminating contact with the feared situation. Thus, according to exposure theorists, it was not necessary to ensure that patients experienced no fear in the presence of the phobic stimulus. Rather, all that was required was to get them into the situation and to prevent them from leaving until the anxiety had diminished on its own.

The extinction theorists were correct and that exposure is at least as effective as systematic desensitisation and is more rapid in its effects. That does not necessarily mean that it is more useful than systematic desensitisation in practice; many patients find exposure therapy very distressing and prefer the kinder, gentler alternative provided by systematic desensitisation. Although exposure typically works more rapidly than does systematic desensitisation, it often takes as long to persuade a patient to try exposure techniques as it does to complete a full course of systematic desensitisation.

Although patients who already have acquired a conditioned fear response will undoubtedly experience distress when exposed to the object of their fears, the fact that they become anxious during the course of that exposure neither facilitates nor retards the extinction process.

Exposure plus response prevention has a clear advantage over systematic desensitisation in the treatment of more complex disorders related to anxiety. It appears to be particularly helpful in the treatment of severe obsessive-compulsive disorder (OCD) and severe agoraphobia. Although systematic desensitisation has had limited success with such severe disorders, the process of constructing and working through the literally dozens of hierarchies required typically makes the approach wildly impractical.

15.4. Conclusion

Unnecessary fears create a lot of mental disorders in people. These phobias affect our normal life adversely. To wither away such causeless fears, we have to pick out the reason behind such phobias. The therapist in this field will help the people with phobias to get rid of such problems.

References

Rapee, R.M., "Overcoming Shyness and Social Phobia", *Chapter 6*, pg. 61-75, passim, Lifestyle Press, 1998.

Richard, David, *Handbook of Exposure Therapies* Imprint: Academic Press, 2006.

16

Genetic Counselling

16.1. Introduction

Human beings inherit some qualities from their parents. This may be positive or negative. The offspring of a singer may become another singer. That is the quality she/he acquire from his/her parents. In such a way, we inherit some bad qualities or diseases also from our parents. Some mental disorders also have the ability to transfer it to the offspring. For treating such mental disorders, parents and relatives of the client also should be gone under treatment. Genetic counselling is the process by which patients or relatives, at risk of an inherited disorder, are advised of the consequences and nature of the disorder, the probability of developing or transmitting it, and the options open to them in management and family planning in order to prevent, avoid or ameliorate it. This complex process can be seen from diagnostic and supportive aspects.

16.2. Treating Methods in Genetic Counselling

Genetic counselling can occur before conception through to adulthood for adult onset genetic conditions such as Huntington's disease or hereditary cancer syndromes.

16.2.1. Beneficiaries of Genetic Counselling

Genetic counselling can be done at any stages of the treatment. Women get counselling before child birth. Genetic counsellors educate the patient about their testing options and inform them of their results. If a prenatal screening or test is abnormal, the genetic counsellor evaluates the risk of an affected pregnancy, educates the patient about these risks and informs the patient of their options.

Even after the birth of a child with a genetic condition, a person may also undergo genetic counselling. In these instances, the genetic counsellor explains the condition to the patient along with recurrence risks in future children. In all cases of a positive family history for a condition, the genetic counsellor can evaluate risks, recurrence and explain the condition itself.

More over, genetic counsellors provide supportive counselling to families, serve as patient advocates and refer individuals and families to community or state support services. They serve as educators and resource people for other health care professionals and for the general public. Some counsellors also work in administrative capacities. Many engage in research activities related to the field of medical genetics and genetic counselling. The field of genetic counselling is rapidly expanding and many counsellors are taking on "non-traditional roles" which includes working for genetic companies and laboratories.

16.2.2. Morality in Genetic Counselling

Genetic counselling is a communication process which deals with human problems associated with the occurrence, or the risk of occurrence of a genetic disorder in a family. This process involves an attempt by one or more appropriately trained persons (genetic counsellors) to help the individual or family to:

(i) Comprehend the medical facts, including the diagnosis, the probable course of the disorder, and the available management,

(ii) Appreciate the way heredity contributes to disorder, and the risk of recurrence in specified relatives,

(iii) Understand the options for dealing with the risk of recurrence,

(iv) Choose the course of action which seems appropriate to them in view of their risk and the family goals and in accordance with the decision, and

(v) Make the best possible adjustment to the disorder in the affected family member and/or the risk of recurrence of that disorder.

Today, genetic counselling goes beyond mere presentations of risk facts and figures to the prevention and cure of disease, the relief of pain and the maintenance of health. For many disorders it is only possible to give precise recurrence risk conditions and also the order of risk.

Moral, ethical and philosophical aspects involved in genetic counselling are now emerging as major issues with the development of the application of various diagnostic techniques as amniocentesis and fetoscopy during pregnancy. The consultee and the counsellor are now faced with choices that were once left to fate.

16.2.3. Prenatal Diagnosis and Abortions

There are a number of issues which question the morality of the society. Prenatal diagnosis and abortions are one of such problems. In India prenatal sex determination is controlled by law. There are a lot of immoral things are happening in the field of child birth. People's preference to boy child disturbs even the sex ratio. Moral problems arise constantly in social life with the need to resolve conflicts between moral rules and principles to help, regulate and modify desires.

When genetic risks are high, the desire to have a healthy child and to avoid danger to oneself, family and society are frequently in conflict. Although 96% of the counselling sessions end well with no or very little chances for the occurrence of the disease, the remaining 4% people in the high risk category are left with three options:

i) Prenatal diagnosis and abortion if required,

ii) Artificial insemination, and

iii) Gene therapy.

The problems of moral choices can be, in decreasing order of frequency and difficulty as:

i) Abortion choices,

ii) Problems related to access and distribution of prenatal diagnosis as a service, and

iii) Problems related to research on prenatal diagnosis (PND).

16.2.3.1 Abortion Choices

Law prevents abortions. The choice to abort any pregnancy is a moral problem wherever duties to protect the interests of the woman, the fetus and the society are held to be in conflict. Historically some of the earliest conflicts about PND were on the question of whether abortion was its primary goal. One group argued that the destruction of certain fetuses was the morally unacceptable goal of PND outweighing the possibility that it might give reassurance to some at-risk parents that their child would (likely) be unaffected. The other group contended that since PND was done largely with intent to abort an affected fetus, the practice contradicted the basic purpose of medicinal science.

The reasons behind the difficulties and dilemmas of abortion choices are:

- The high moral status of the woman carrying the foetus at mid-trimester,
- The wide spectrum of severity in some diagnosable genetic disorders,
- The treatability of some disorders,
- The possibility of diagnosing twins where one is affected and the other healthy, claims that the practice of mid-trimester abortion creates a precedence for paediatric/ euthanasia, selective abortion, and
- Decisions about treatment of handicapped newborns.

With the involvement of euthenics, i.e. state-of-the-art of treatment for genetic disorders by modification of the environment to allow the genetically abnormal individual to develop normally and to live a relatively normal life, abortion choices will become predictably more complicated. Euthenics can be applied both medically and socially - examples of phenylketourea (PKU) treatment by diet control, use of human growth hormone for growth disorders, purified factor VIII for haemophilia A, etc., illustrate medical euthenics, while special schools for deaf children, illustrate social euthenics.

16.2.3.2 Access to PND Service

The central moral problem in medical ethics is the access to and distribution of PND and genetic services. Except for Denmark where about 80% of the women who need PND receive it, most of the countries do not meet the true need for services. Further, women who undergo PND belong largely to higher economic groups. Lack of financial resources and adequate planning has restricted the distribution of genetic services in almost every country.

16.2.3.3. Research on PND

Research in the context of clinical trials raises ethical issues. A randomised clinical trial requires careful consideration because a proven new approach will be withheld by chance, from some in order to compare its advantages and disadvantages. Clinical research in prenatal or prenatal care presents special complexities because the foetus, as well as the pregnant woman, are the subject of research.

16.3. Ethical Problems

Counselling is an understanding of a set of facts according to the counsellors' frame of reference, background in the science of genetics, and previous training and experience in effectively communicating with the consultee. In order to communicate effectively, the counsellor must consider the educational background of the consultee, what to disclose and how to limit the ways in which he can communicate. It has been found that the principal obstacles to the effective use of genetic counselling are emotional conflicts, and lack of knowledge of genetics and biology.

The biggest hurdle before the counsellor is presenting his knowledge in an unbiased manner. It is difficult for a counsellor to impart unbiased information because of the consultee's personal and family history such as parental age, ethnic background, reproductive history, i.e. abortions, stillborn or dead siblings, and the age, sex and health of the living children. This may lead the counsellor to adopt a directive rather than a non-directive approach to genetic counselling.

The major difference between directive and non-directive counselling is whether or not the counsellor actively participates or helps the consultees to make a decision. Directive counselling has a positive influence on the consultee's decision. The non-directive approach involves presentation of the facts in an unbiased manner, leaving the entire responsibility of decision with the consultee. Counsellors can be and have been fooled with respect to certain inherited conditions because of improper measurements and observations and/or because of similar symptoms of many genetic diseases.

The counsellor probably cannot completely disassociate himself from his own values and present the information in such a way that the recipient is not completely free to make his own judgement. In interpreting the probability even for a single gene disease, the counsellor, depending on his level of personal emotional involvement in the particular case, may bias or slant the data. The counsellor may not change the truth but his tone, manner of speech and other facial and body gestures can influence the information transfer.

During counselling, the counsellor may come across other findings, that may put him in a situation of ethical dilemma. Some of these are foetal sex, findings of questionable or potentially harmful significance, false paternity, etc. Occasionally, disputes arise about the significance of laboratory findings especially about the true v/s pseudomosaicism or by possibility of contamination by maternal cells. The issue is whether the disclosure of a finding of probably small significance will result in severe parental anxiety leading to psychological problems.

Males and females with normal phenotypes who are discovered to have XX or XY chromosomal complement, respectively. Many families have some secretes to conceal. The medical geneticists learn these secrets, such as previous abortions, previous abnormal births, and occasional false paternity. The findings can be made after PND of a recessive disorder and testing the carrier parents or in the context of genetic screening after the birth of an affected infant. The putative father believes that he must be a carrier, but tests are negative. The option left is partial or total deception.

16.3.1. Ethical Direction in Genetic Counselling

The proposal for guidelines for PND, genetic counselling and screening assumes that consensus exists among medical geneticists, obstetricians and parents about some key ethical principles and approaches to difficult choices:

i) Parental autonomy in abortion choices;

ii) Non-directive counselling;

iii) PND that must be provided when parents need the information to prepare themselves for the birth of a possibly affected child;

iv) Practitioners need to disclose to the consultee the risks and benefits of each procedure in PND;

v) Information of XY females and XX males with great care that casts no ambiguity on the patient's social and phenotypic sexual identity;

vi) In case putative father is not the biological father of the foetus, the mother to be informed first to avoid social problems and she may be left to take final decision;

vii) Medical geneticists to decide which of the disorders warrants the options of prenatal diagnosis and termination of pregnancy, and

viii) Consequences from the above to be evaluated in terms of basic ethical principles, and critical tests of what is best for the individuals, groups and society.

16.4. Conclusion

Genetic counselling is a practical method of calculating risk figures, intended for information regarding the unborn, and we ought to use it in an efficient manner but in a direction, which our ethics and morality point to. The decision taken by the parents after the counselling session must leave them satisfied instead of placing them in a state of dilemma.

References

Applebaum, E. G., and Firestein, S. K., *A Genetic Counseling Casebook,* New York: Free Press, 1983.

Baker, D. L.; Schette, J. L.; and Uhlmann, W. R., *A Guide to Genetic Counselling,* New York: Wiley-Liss, 1998.

Ferrell, J., "Genetic Counseling", *Vogue,* February, 1992.

Harper, P. S., and Clarke, A., *Genetics, Society, and Clinical Practice,* Oxford: BIOS Scientific; Herndon: Distributors, USA and Canada, BIOS Scientific, 1997.

Kelly, P. T., *Dealing with Dilemma: A Manual for Genetic Counselors,* New York: Springer-Verlag, 1977.

Kessler, S., ed., *Genetic Counseling: Psychological Dimensions,* New York: Academic Press, 1979.

Otten, A. L., "Parental Agony: How Counselors Guide Couples When Science Spots Genetic Risks." *The Wall Street Journal,* March 8, 1989.

Shiloh, S., "Genetic Counselling: A Developing Area of Interest for Psychologists", *Professional Psychology: Research and Practice,* 1996.

17

Psychoeducation

17.1. Introduction

Peaceful and happy life is a dream for all human beings. A deviation from this normal flow of life disturbs the mental peace. When behavioural or psychological difficulties arise, people need specific information about what is happening—the diagnosis, the meaning of specific symptoms, what is known about the causes, effects, and implications of the problem in question. The more family and friends know, the less they will blame the person who is experiencing it, or themselves for thinking they had somehow caused it.

While the behaviour of an individual becomes frightening and bizarre, the family that person belongs to needs help. The families also seek help for understanding the reason behind the person denies that anything is wrong, why there is resistance to taking medications or being hospitalised, and why very often the family itself is blamed by the patient and health care professionals. Families need timely, basic education about the painful and long-term effects.

Families need information on management and coping skills; information about why certain medications are being used and their side effects; an understanding of the reasons and implications for noncompliance with prescriptions or following through with recommended treatment.

Psychoeducation is the education of a person in subject areas that serve the goals of treatment and rehabilitation. It involves teaching people about their problem, how to treat it, and how to recognise signs of relapse so that they can get necessary treatment before their difficulty worsens or occurs again. Family psychoeducation includes teaching coping strategies and problem-solving skills to families, friends, and/or caregivers to help them deal more effectively with the individual.

Psychoeducational training involves patients with schizophrenia, clinical depression, anxiety disorders, psychotic illnesses, eating disorders, and personality disorders, as well as patient training courses in the context of the treatment of physical illnesses. Family members are also included. A goal is for the patient to understand and be better able to deal with the presented illness. Also, the patient's own strengths, resources and coping skills are reinforced, in order to avoid relapse and contribute to their own health and wellness on a long-term basis. The theory is, with better knowledge the patient has of their illness, the better the patient can live with their condition.

Since it is often difficult for the patient and their family members to accept the patient's diagnosis, psychoeducation also has the function of contributing to the destigmatisation of psychological disturbances and to diminish barriers to treatment. Through an improved view of the causes and the effects of the illness, psychoeducation frequently broadens the patient's view of their illness and this increased understanding can positively affect the patient. The relapse risk is in this way lowered; patients and family members, who are more well-informed about the disease, feel less helpless. Important elements in the Psychoeducation are:

— Information transfer (symptomatology of the disturbance, causes, treatment concepts etc)

— Emotional discharge (understanding to promote, exchange of experiences with others concerning, contacts etc)

— Support of a medication or psychotherapeutic treatment, as co-operation is promoted between the mental health professional and patient.

— Assistance to self-help (e.g. training, as crisis situations are promptly recognised and which steps then to be undertaken to be able to help the patient)

People should be aware about their mental illness. Psychoeducation is not a treatment. It is designed to be part of an overall treatment plan. Knowledge of one's illness is crucial for individuals and their support network to be able to design their own relapse prevention plans and strategies.

The more a person is aware of their illness and how it affects their own lives and that of others, the more control that person has over their illness. This means that, with appropriate knowledge and techniques, episodes of mental illness occur less often and are usually less severe in intensity and duration.

17.2. Features of Psychoeducation

Treatment models that have been supported by evidence of effectiveness have required clinicians to adhere to fifteen principles in working with families of persons who have mental illness:

- Coordinate all elements of treatment and rehabilitation to ensure that everyone is working toward the same goals in a collaborative, supportive relationship.
- Pay attention to both the social and the clinical needs of the consumer.
- Provide optimum medication management.
- Listen to families' concerns and involve them as equal partners in the planning and delivery of treatment.
- Explore family members' expectations of the treatment programme and expectations for the consumer.
- Assess the strengths and limitations of the family's ability to support the consumer.
- Help resolve family conflict by responding sensitively to emotional distress.
- Address feelings of loss.
- Provide relevant information for the consumer and his or her family at appropriate times.
- Provide an explicit crisis plan and professional response.
- Help improve communication among family members.
- Provide training for the family in structured problem-solving techniques.
- Encourage family members to expand their social support networks

— Be flexible in meeting the needs of the family.

— Provide the family with easy access to another professional in the event that the current work with the family ceases.

Psychoeducation can be provided in single-family and multi-family groups. For multi-family groups, practitioners invite five to six consumers and their families to participate in a psychoeducation group for at least six months. Additional meeting time promotes improved outcomes. Meetings are held every other week. The format is structured and pragmatic to assist people with developing skills for handling problems posed by mental illness. Over time practitioners, family members, and consumers form a partnership as they work toward recovery. Consumers and their supporters may decide to meet as a single family rather than in the multi-family group format.

17.3. Individual and Group Psychoeducation

People can acquire knowledge about the psychological disorders either by individually or by group. In the groups several patients are informed about their illnesses at once. Also, exchanges of experience between the concerned patients and mutual support play a role in the healing process.

17.3.1. Methods

A thorough understanding about the illness helps person an easy withdrawal. Psychoeducation works by improving the knowledge patients and their families have and providing a greater understanding of the importance and benefits of medication. Families are encouraged to keep a journal of pertinent information so they have a reference to consult.

Information about the illness helps people to take necessary actions on medication, prognosis, alleviating and aggravating factors. Early signs of relapse are described and actively monitored. Families are helped to understand how high expressed emotion environments can perhaps help to maintain or aggravate symptoms. This crucial information allows families to plan and adapt around the reality of prolonged emotional or behavioural difficulty; it enables them to put the situation into perspective and to begin to modify their own lives as necessary. Participants are taught skills that change their lifestyle, enhance their therapy and assist them to live more productive and fulfilled lives.

Family psychoeducation reduces distress, confusion, and anxiety within the family, which may in turn help the individual recover. Children, adolescents and adults learn skills that will complement their therapy and may reduce the use of more costly treatment modalities. Eleven or more individual psycho-educational sessions were significantly more effective than treatment alone in preventing relapse at 9-18 months. Brief group psychoeducation was also more effective than treatment alone in preventing relapse or readmission to hospital by 1 year. Combining the results from all trials, relapse rates at 9-18 months' follow up were significantly lower in the psychoeducation group than in the control group.

Psychoeducation in combination with medication has been used successfully in relation to people with schizophrenia, bipolar disorder, attention-deficit/hyperactivity disorder (ADHD), and depression, as well as assisting their family and caregivers. People being treated for, or who are attempting to prevent depression, often require ongoing assistance to change their behavior and life style.

17.3.2. Risks and Side Effects

Acutely sick patients are frequently overtaxed with schizophrenic psychosis, and they suffer from substantial thinking, concentration and attention disturbances, at the beginning of their illness. Care should be taken not to overwhelm the patient with too much information. Besides positive effects of a therapeutic measure like Psychoeducation, in principle, also other possible risks should be considered.

The detailed knowledge of the illness, in particular regarding chances of recovery, therapy possibilities and the disease process can make the patient and/or family member stressed. Therefore, one should draw an exact picture of the risks regarding the psychological condition of the patient. It should be considered how much the patient already understands, and how much knowledge the patient can take up and process in their current condition.

The ability to concentrate should be considered as well as the maximum level of emotional stress that the patient can take. In the context of a Psychoeducational programme a selection of aspects and/or therapy possibilities can be considered and discussed with the patient. Otherwise, the patient may form an incomplete picture of their illness, and they may form ideas about treatment alternatives from a vantage point of incomplete information. However, the professional should also make a complete representation of the possibilities of treatment, and attention should be paid to not make excessive demands of the patient, i.e. giving too much information at once.

17.4. Family Psychoeducation

It is a method based on clinical findings for training families to work together with mental health professionals as part of an overall clinical treatment plan for their family members. Family psychoeducation has been shown to improve patient outcomes for persons with schizophrenia and other major mental illnesses.

The members in a family and other individuals involved in the lives and care of adults who have serious mental illnesses often provide emotional support, case management, financial assistance, advocacy, and housing to their mentally ill loved ones. Although serving in this capacity can be rewarding, it may be very difficult. Family members often have limited access to the resources and information they need. Research conducted over the past decade has shown that patients' outcomes improve when the needs of family members for information, clinical guidance, and support are met.

There are a number of evolve to address the needs of families of persons with mental illness: individual consultation and family psychoeducation conducted by a mental health professional, various forms of more traditional family therapy, and a range of professionally led short-term family education programmes, sometimes referred to as therapeutic education. However, the term "psychoeducation" can be misleading: family psychoeducation includes many therapeutic elements, often uses a consultative framework, and shares characteristics with other types of family interventions.

Over the past two decades, mental health care professionals have developed a variety of family psychoeducation programmes. These programmes have been offered as part of an overall clinical treatment plan for individuals who have mental illness. They last nine months to five years, are usually diagnosis specific, and focus primarily on consumer outcomes, although the well-being of the family is an essential intermediate outcome. Family psychoeducation models differ in their format-for example, multiple-family, single-family, or mixed sessions-the duration of treatment, consumer participation, location-for example, clinic based, home, family practice, or other community settings-and the degree of emphasis on didactic, cognitive-behavioral, and systemic techniques.

17.4.1. Objectives

Psychoeducation help to prevent patients with severe mental illnesses from relapsing, and to promote their re-entry into their home communities, with particular regard for their social and occupational functioning. Family psychoeducation programmes seek to provide families with the information they need about mental illness and the coping skills that will help them deal with their loved one's psychiatric disorder. Family psychoeducation has been shown to be effective for all families who have contact with a relative who has mental illness.

Family psychoeducation is effective for consumers with mental illness and other problems, especially consumers who have been hospitalised. Consumers with a variety of diagnosis have benefited from family psychoeducation:

— Schizophrenia
— Schizoaffective disorder
— Bipolar illness
— Major depression
— Borderline personality disorder

The members of family education can be anyone who is helping and/or supporting a consumer in his or her recovery—parents, other relatives, close friends, or neighbours. The consumer and family do not have to live in the same house or apartment

Families experience many burdens (financial, social, and psychological) in serving as long-term caregivers for their loved ones. Although the primary focus of family psychoeducation groups is improved patient outcomes, an essential intermediate goal is to promote the well-being of the family.

Family psychoeducation consists of several different models. Although they include many common elements, these different models include: single- and multiple-family groups; mixed groups that include family members and consumers (patients); groups of varying duration ranging from nine months to more than five years; and groups that focus on patients and families at different phases in the illness.

Multi-family groups, which bring together several patients and their families, lead to better outcomes than single-family psychoeducation groups. The origins of multiple-family group therapy go back as far as 1960, when these groups were first assembled to solve ward-management problems in a psychiatric hospital. Lasting a minimum of nine months, the programmes provided their participants with information about mental illness, its symptoms and treatment; medication and its side effects; how to communicate with a person with mental illness; and techniques for crisis intervention and mutual problem-solving.

17.5. Conclusion

A person should be aware about his/her illness for an effective treatment. If they are aware, they respond positively towards medicines and it help to recover very soon. This is also same in the mental treatment also. Knowledge about the illness a person suffers helps them to take adequate measures towards treatment.

References

Lefley, Harriet P. and Dale L. Johnson, eds., *Family Interventions in Mental Illness: International Perspectives*, Westport, CT: Praeger Publishers, 2002.

McFarlane, William R., "Families, Patients and Clinicians as Partners: Clinical Strategies and Research Outcomes in Single- and Multiple-Family Psychoeducation," In *Helping Families Cope with Mental Illness*, Switzerland: Harwood Academic Publishers, 1994.

Bibliography

Abramowitz, C. V., "The effectiveness of group psychotherapy with children", *Archives of General Psychiatry,* 1980.

Agazarian, Y., *Systems-centered therapy for groups,* New York: Guilford Press, 1997.

Applebaum, E. G., and Firestein, S. K., *A Genetic Counseling Casebook,* New York: Free Press, 1983.

Axline, V.M., *Play therapy: The inner dynamics of childhood,* Cambridge, MA: Houghton Mifflin, 1947.

Baker, D. L.; Schette, J. L.; and Uhlmann, W. R., *A Guide to Genetic Counselling,* New York: Wiley-Liss, 1998.

Bauer, G. P., & Kobos, J. C., *Brief psychotherapy: Short-term psychodynamic intervention,* Northvale, NJ: J, 1987.

Blum, S. R., "Ethical issues in managed mental health", In S. Feldman (Ed.), *Managed mental health services,* Springfield, IL: Charles C. Thomas, 1992.

Boss, M., "Anxiety, Guilt and Psychotherapeutic Liberation" *Review of Existential Psychology and Psychiatry,* Vol 11, no.3, Sept. 1962.

Budman, S. H., & Gurman, A. S., *Theory and practice of brief psychotherapy,* New York: Guilford Press, 1988.

Burgin, Victor, James Donald and Cora Kaplan, eds., *Formations of Fantasy,* Routledge, 1989.

Casey, R. J., & Berman, J. S., "The outcome of psychotherapy with children", *Psychological Bulletin,* 1985.

Christophersen, E. R., & Mortweet, S. L., "Treatments that work with children: Empirically supported strategies for managing childhood problems", Washington, DC: American Psychological Association, 2001.

Clarizio, H. F., & McCoy, G. F., *Behavior disorders in children* (3rd ed.), New York: HarperCollins, 1983.

Cohn, H., *Existential Thought and Therapeutic Practice,* London: Sage, 1997.

Corey, M.S., & Corey, G., *Groups: Process and practice* (5th ed.), Pacific Grove, CA: Brooks/Cole, 1997.

Cramer-Azima, F. & Richmond, L.H. (ed), *Adolescent Group Psychotherapy (monograph),* American Group Psychotherapy Association.

Deurzen E. van., *Existential Counselling in Practice,* London: Sage Publications, 2nd edition 2002.

Dewald, Paul, M.D., "The Psychoanalytic Psychotherapies." In *Textbook of Psychoanalysis,* edited by Edward Nersessian, M.D. and Richard G. Kopff, M.D. Washington, DC: American Psychiatric Press, 1996.

Dryden, Windy & Mytton, Jill, *Four Approaches to Counselling & Psychotherapy*, London & New York: Routledge, 1999.

Ellis, Albert, Mike Abrams and Lidia Abrams, *Personality Theories: Critical Perspectives,* New York: Sage Press, 2008.

Erickson, M. T., *Behavior disorders of children and adolescents: Assessment, etilogy, and intervention,* (3rd ed.). Englewood Cliffs, NJ: Prentice-Hall, 1997.

Erikson, E. H., *Childhood and society* (2nd ed.), New York: Norton, 1963.

Feltham, Colin, *What Is Counselling?*, 1995.

Ferrell, J., "Genetic Counseling", *Vogue,* February, 1992.

Friedman, W. H., *Referring patients for group psychotherapy: Some guidelines,* Hospital & Community Psychiatry, 1976.

Froggatt, Wayne, *A Brief Introduction To Rational Emotive Behaviour Therapy,* Third Edition, New Zealand Centre for Cognitive Behaviour Therapy, 2005.

Geraty, R. D., Hendren, R. L., & Flaa, C. J., "Ethical perspectives on managed care as it relates to child and adolescent psychiatry", *Journal of the American Academy of Child and Adolescent Psychiatry,* 1992.

Gladding, S. T., *Counseling: A Comprehensive Profession*, Third Edition, 1996.

Grunebaum, H. & Kates, W., "Whom to refer for group psychotherapy", *American Journal of Psychiatry,* 1977

Harper, P. S., and Clarke, A., *Genetics, Society, and Clinical Practice,* Oxford: BIOS Scientific; Herndon: Distributors, USA and Canada, BIOS Scientific, 1997.

Henin, A., Warman, M., & Kendall, P. C., "Cognitive-behavioral therapy with children and adolescents", In G. Simos (Ed.) *Cognitive behavior therapy: A guide for the practicing clinician,* East Sussex: Brunner-Routledge, 2002.

Juliet Mitchell and Jacqueline Rose (eds.), *Feminine Sexuality and the Ecole Freudienne,* Macmillan, 1982.

Kelly, P. T., *Dealing with Dilemma: A Manual for Genetic Counselors,* New York: Springer-Verlag, 1977.

Kendall, P. C., Choudhury, M., Chung, H., & Robin, J., "Cognitive-behavioral approaches", In M. Lewis (Ed.) *Child and adolescent psychiatry* (3(rd) ed.), Baltimore, MD: Lippincott Williams & Wilkins. 2002.

Kessler, S., ed., *Genetic Counseling: Psychological Dimensions,* New York: Academic Press, 1979.

Kjell Raaheim, Janek Wankowski & John Radford, *Helping Students to Learn: Teaching, Counselling, Research* (rev. 2nd ed.). Buckingham/Bristol, PA: Society for Research into Higher Education and Open University Press, 1991.

Klerman, Gerald L., and others, *Interpersonal Psychotherapy of Depression,* New York: Basic Books, Inc., 1984.

Lacan, Jacques, "Seminar XI: Four Fundamental Concepts of Psychoanalysis", *Trans. Alan Sheridan,* Penguin, 1986.

Landreth, G.L., *Play therapy: The art of the relationship,* Munice, IN: Accelerated Development, 1991.

Laplanche, J. and J.-B. Pontalis, *The Language of Psychoanalysis,* London: Hogarth, 1973.

Lebow, J., "Guidelines for Conducting Couple and Family Therapy", In G. Koocker, J.C. Norcross, & S.S. Hill (eds.), *Psychologists Desk Reference (2 nd edition.),* New York: Oxford Press, 2004

Lefley, Harriet P. and Dale L. Johnson, eds., *Family Interventions in Mental Illness: International Perspectives,* Westport, CT: Praeger Publishers, 2002.

Malekoff, A., *Group Work with Adolescents, Principles and Practice,* N.Y., Guilford Press, 1997.

McFarlane, William R., "Families, Patients and Clinicians as Partners: Clinical Strategies and Research Outcomes in Single- and Multiple-Family Psychoeducation," In *Helping Families Cope with Mental Illness,* Switzerland: Harwood Academic Publishers, 1994.

Merry, Tony and Lusty, Bob, *What is Person-Centered Counselling? A Personal and Practical Guide,* Essex: Gale Centre Publications, 1993.

O'Leary, E. and Keane N., "Person-Centered Therapy", in P. Hawkins and I. Nesteros *Perspectives in Psychology,* Athens: Ellinka Grammata, 1997.

Olsen, D. P., "The ethical considerations of managed care in mental health treatment", *Journal of Psychosocial Nursing*, 1994.

Otten, A. L., "Parental Agony: How Counselors Guide Couples When Science Spots Genetic Risks." *The Wall Street Journal*, March 8, 1989.

Pinsof, W., "A Shamanic Tapesty: My Experiences with Individual, Marital, and Family Therapy", In Geller, J.D., Norcross, J.C. and Orlinsky, D.E. (Eds.), *The Psychotherapist's Own Psychotherapy: Patient and Clinician Perspectives*, New York: Oxford University Press, 2004

Powdermaker, F. & Frank, J. *Group Psychotherapy: Studies in Methodology of Research and Therapy*, Cambridge MA: Harvard University Press, 1953.

Price, J. R., Hescheles, D. R., & Price, A. R. (Eds.), *A guide to starting psychotherapy groups*, San Diego: Academic Press, 1999.

Prochaska, James O., and John C. Norcross, *Systems of Psychotherapy: A Transtheoretical Analysis*, 4th edition, Pacific Grove: Brooks/Cole Publishing Company, 1999.

Rapee, R.M., "Overcoming Shyness and Social Phobia", *Chapter 6*, pg. 61-75, passim, Lifestyle Press, 1998.

Richard, David, *Handbook of Exposure Therapies* Imprint: Academic Press, 2006.

Rogers, C.R., *Counselling and Psychotherapy: New Concepts in Practice*, Boston: Houghton Mifflin, 1942.

Rose, S.R., *Group Work with Children and Adolescents: Prevention and Intervention in School and Community System*, London, Sage Pub, 1998.

Shiloh, S., "Genetic Counselling: A Developing Area of Interest for Psychologists", *Professional Psychology: Research and Practice*, 1996.

Simon, N. P., "Practitioner ethics and managed care", *Managed Care Quarterly*, 1994.

Sue Wheeler & Jan Birtle, *A Handbook for Personal Tutors*, Buckingham/ Bristol, PA: Society for Research into Higher Education and Open University Press, 1993.

Wineburgh, M., "Ethics, managed care, and outpatient psychotherapy", *Clinical Social Work Journal*, 1998.

Wolff, M.; Krefman, K. and Martin, P., "Maintaining or Enhancing Couple and Family Relationships in the Face of Dementia", *Buehler Center on Aging Magazine*, Summer, 2004.

Yalom Irving, His book *Love's Executioner and Other Tales of Psychotherapy*, 1989.

Index